FOREWORD BY MAJ. GEN. JOSEPH J. SKAFF

BUDAPEST TO VIETNAM

COL. NICHOLAS J. HUN
AND MICHAEL L. JEWELL

ISBN# 978-1-0879-5631-2
Nicholas J. Hun, Author
Michael L. Jewell, Co-author
Proofread by Krystle Berg
Formatted by Michael L. Jewell
Cover Design by Jay Cookingham
Special thanks to Nancy Jewell-Holverson
for transcribing audio material
Printed in the United States of America

Excerpt from ***BUDAPEST TO VIETNAM***

"The chatter of the enemy was getting much too close, and we were receiving some "incoming" from the tree line about 75 yards out. It was time to break contact with them, but first, to "get some" before departing.

"I took the M79 from the striker next to me and zeroed in on the tree line where the bushes showed some movement. I was experienced firing the old M20 (3.5 inch) bazooka in training with the 1st Airborne Battle Group of the 187th Infantry at Fort Bragg, making the conversion to the M79 fairly easy.

"Having a relatively free line of fire, I shot the M79 toward the enemy three times. The first round impacted long and the second one short. This established a bracket around the target, allowing me to place the final round with deadly accuracy. As I fired one more time, the HE (high explosive) round landed just as four or five NVA soldiers, with AK and SKS rifles at the ready, stepped proudly out of the heavy jungle into the tall grass.

"We heard them scream and watched them fall, helmets flying like Frisbees, as they were instantly blown up in a haze of gray smoke. Departing, I turned one last time to witness their throes of death in the smoking elephant grass."

DEDICATION

To Brenda, my wife of fifty years, the sage of the classroom, who has enhanced learning of her elementary school charges for over two decades.

ଔ

To our daughter Tara Hun Dorris, and son, Doctor Nick C. Hun, who continue to improve lives, and health through research and practice as Medical Professionals.

ଔ

Finally, to my siblings Laszlo Hun, Ilona Farkas, and Maria Horansky, who have been there through thick and thin with their unwavering love and support.

TABLE OF CONTENTS

FOREWORD BY MAJOR GENERAL JOSEPH J. SKAFF

Colonel Nick Hun had over three decades of dedicated service in the United State Army. His distinguished service as a soldier and leader included combat tours with the Special Forces. His contributions in law enforcement with the military police in command positions was equally outstanding. His service was demonstrated by his exemplary duty to his soldiers and the Nation, always placing the needs of his soldiers above all else.

Upon his retirement from active military service, he continued his public service in the State of West Virginia. I was most fortunate to be the recipient of his many years of experience in law enforcement at a critical time in the State's criminal justice system. Our correctional system was in immediate need of an experienced proven leader in corrections and law enforcement.

Nick served as the senior advisor to the West Virginia National Guard under my tenure as the Adjutant General. I was very much aware of his capabilities to tackle the difficult problems facing our corrections system. Upon my recommendation to the Governor of West Virginia, Nick was appointed Commissioner of Corrections. This was a time when the main prison in the State was in shambles and a new replacement was in the process of opening. Thanks to his leadership and expertise, the difficult issues were addressed and eventually resolved. His tenure as Commissioner was outstanding, and I was most fortunate and grateful to have Nick work for me within the Department of Military and Public Safety during this critical time.

WHO PACKED MY PARACHUTE?

Charles Plumb, naval aviator, and author of *I'M NO HERO,* was shot down over the jungles of Vietnam. When he ejected from his aircraft, happily, his parachute worked, allowing him to make a safe landing. Afterwards, he spent six years in a POW camp. Years later, Plumb was honored to meet the man who had actually packed the parachute he wore on that terrible day. Now, as a motivational speaker, he talks about his life in terms of those who have helped him along the way by *packing his parachute!*

While serving for six years in various airborne units in the US Army, I had never thought much about the men and women who packed my parachutes, allowing me to survive those jumps. These individuals, who go unnoticed in their seemingly mundane tasks of existence, are indispensable to the life and death equation of jumping from an aircraft in flight. Similarly, such people exist throughout our society in coaching, counseling, medicine, and hundreds of other places, "packing our parachutes."

I have often thought about the many people whose timely help changed the course of events in my life. I am particularly referring to those who contributed to any success I might have had as an army officer and later in the various things I did related to my military service. Their style of altruism and generosity is the fiber that keeps our society intact and thriving. Their acts of selfless benevolence must be gratefully acknowledged, even if belatedly.

Accordingly, I will endeavor to recognize these individuals by name in this book as a matter of honor, respect, and gratitude. Where certain people have been hurtful and less than kind, I will mention some of those events as well in passing without name, as they also had an important part in who I am today—***Nick Hun***

TRAIN OUT OF BUDAPEST

As World War II raged across Europe, I was born the second son of Laszlo and Ilona Hun in Budapest, Hungary on January 26, 1942. Our father, who was in the Hungarian Army reserve, was away fighting the Russians along the Eastern Front. Wounded in the Battle for Budapest in 1945, and perhaps because he had blue eyes and blond hair, the Germans took him along and dropped him off at a hospital in Austria. When my mother got the news, she packed up my older brother Laszlo Jr, sister Ilona, and myself and departed Hungary by train to become refugees in Germany. My youngest sister, Marika, would be born there later in May of 1950.

My father was later reunited with our family in Germany. Sadly, his left arm had been amputated after being shattered by five rounds from a Kalashnikov rifle.

Many of Europe's bombed-out cities were predominantly without infrastructure. I had to grow up among the ruins and rubble of these shattered buildings, the results of several years of continuous pounding by allied aircraft.

My older brother Laszlo and I played here on the streets, often littered with the bodies of dead animals and sometimes people. As children often do, we brothers found ways to amuse ourselves, sometimes playing "cowboys and Indians" amidst the debris of the war. Our improvised "playground" was extremely hazardous due to unexploded bombs and live grenades left strewn upon the ground by retreating German soldiers.

During this time, I had the occasion to observe the American soldiers who were busy mopping up the remnants of the German army, many of them surrendering, not aware that the war was now over. I was surprised to see the GIs do their jobs and at the same time, dispense benevolence with a smile. As I watched these tough Americans patrolling in their jeeps with their Thompson submachine guns at the ready, little did I know, that one day, I would also carry a Thompson and many other weapons to fight for the greatest nation on earth.

Sometimes, German soldiers would approach my brother and I as we played among the spent cartridges and other wreckage from the war, asking us if the GIs were taking surrendered prisoners. Our standard boyish response was always, "They are the good guys; they give us candy!"

I quickly realized, even as a young child, that these Americans were different somehow from other soldiers, able to carry a sword in one hand and gifts of kindness in the other. I wanted to become one of them someday, and this became my dream. As a skinny street urchin from war-torn Europe, living with my family in penury, I thought how amazing to be a soldier in the United States Army.

. . .

It was 1946, and my family struggled to settle down to what life had handed us. Little did we know, that before it was over, we would spend the next seven years moving from camp to camp around Germany in places like Memmingen, Kempten, Oberammergau, Augsburg, and Munich.

Each new move brought new challenges for us. My mother washed and ironed clothes and uniforms for the American soldiers. Father, with the help of the family, made furniture out of bamboo to be sold at open-air markets akin to farmer's markets in the United States.

Refugees were particularly unwelcome in Germany due to the scarcity of resources. This sentiment was sometimes expressed by the derogatory term, "dreckige Auslander," (dirty foreigners). This helped make fights among kids more common, and my brother, Laszlo, became an accomplished brawler out of necessity. I also learned how to fight as my dad would send me out to help when Laszlo had to fight several boys at one time.

This scenario continued even in the 1950s in the States, where we were referred to as DPs or "displaced persons." As I got older, I became an efficient fighter, albeit a reluctant one. My friends, from the St. Margaret's of Hungary Elementary School in Cleveland, still talk about those days as if I was a real tough guy.

Laszlo, older than me by two-and-a-half years, played a large part in my life during our teenage years. While we loved each other, as we do now, that never stopped us from duking it out.

One day, on the way to school, we argued; so, Laszlo stopped the car to teach me a lesson. Rather than take a beating, but not wanting to kill my brother, I stabbed him in the thigh with a hunting knife I carried in my boot. There was no school for us that day, rather, it was hospital time to get him sewed up. I think he got the point. That was our last fight!

MY BROTHER 1LT LASZLO HUN WITH THE 11TH US ARMY SPECIAL FORCES RESERVE
INSET PHOTO—LASZLO AS A WASHINGTON D.C. POLICE OFFICER

RESTLESS IN CLEVELAND

Cleveland, Ohio in the early 1950s had an ethnic mix that included many European groups who departed their native lands for the United States after World Wars I and II. Many Eastern Europeans also emigrated here, fleeing the Hungarian revolution of 1956, primarily establishing themselves in the east side of town.

As the coalfields of West Virginia, Kentucky, and Virginia modernized and alternative fuels lessened the demand for this "black gold," out-of-work, white southerners moved to Cleveland, gravitating to the west side of town to find their opportunities there.

Many African Americans, the sons and daughters of sharecroppers and segregation, also migrated here to take advantage of the industrialized North and improve their lot.

These various ethnic groups served to give old Cleveland a particular richness. To walk down Buckeye Road in those days was to see butcher shops, bakeries, and bars from 116th to 130th Street with Gypsy music blaring to well past midnight. Cleveland became a haven for these folks seeking to escape war and poverty. It was truly the spirit of Americana at its best.

Shaker Square, located in a neighborhood of modest two-story houses, had a rapid transit system on rails that could easily take you west to downtown Cleveland or east to Shaker Heights. This journey, thrilling for a young Hungarian boy like myself and his siblings, would transport us past well-appointed mansions and far out of the way into the countryside.

As a young teenager, my friends and I would often ride the transit east to the end of the line and hitchhike another twenty miles to the Chagrin Valley Country Club. Serving as caddies for the more affluent members of society, this could earn us as much as five dollars for a double "loop," or two bags for 18 holes. On busy weekends, golfers might get in 36 holes, leaving us teens flush with newfound wealth.

It was not all work, however, as there were ponds to fish, cards to play, and other mischief for young boys to get into. Lawn mowers and tractors used by the maintenance workers to keep the golf course properly manicured were always fair game to bored caddies waiting for a loop.

One day, I met a pretty young girl named Gail riding her horse by the golf course. My stellar pickup line was, "Nice horse!" *What young lady equestrian would not respond positively to such imaginative verbiage?*

Gail lived with her parents and older sister, Judy, in a home with a pond and stables near the sixteenth tee. My new friend and I enjoyed our walks together among the flowers, serene woods, and meadows. Sweet, innocent and bucolic, these warm, humid days of summer only lasted until late August. Now there would be other things to draw me away such as football practice at John Adams High School back on the east side.

Gail's farewell note to me sadly read, "Watching you go back to school was like having someone go into the army." Little did she and I realize that this little statement would become a harbinger for my future.

. . .

Upon my graduation from John Adams High School in January of 1961, I received calls from several small Ohio colleges regarding football scholarships. However, as my family was relatively poor, I chose not to pursue college at that time, but rather accepted a position as dishwasher at Stouffer's Restaurant on Shaker Square. This establishment belonged to the same folks who owned the famous Stouffer's frozen food and hotel chain. Anyway, this decision on my part was much to the disappointment of my coaches.

At Stouffer's, I found myself quickly promoted to busboy and waiter within three weeks. Uncomfortable, however, with my meteoric rise in the business world, I decided to leave my $40 dollar a week job for the US Army.

Although my wages were to drop to $79 dollars a month, I happily went off to basic training at Fort Knox, Kentucky and then later to Military Police school at Fort Gordon, Georgia.

FORT BRAGG AND JUMP SCHOOL

I arrived at Fort Bragg near Fayetteville, North Carolina on a Saturday in June of 1961. The night ride by Greyhound bus from Fort Gordon after graduation from Military Police school was uneventful enough for this nineteen-year-old and his seven trainee companions. However, what awaited us upon arrival at the segregated Fayetteville bus station was an experience long to be remembered by me and many other aspiring paratroopers of that era.

There were eight of us: Victor, a fellow Clevelander; his friend, Plutchuck, from Detroit; Link, from Texas; Petterson, from Minnesota; Hart, from Montana, along with Johnson and Williams, two black soldiers from the northeast.

Further adding to our misery and segregation, being the order of the day, no white-owned hotel would accommodate our racially mixed group of soldiers. We then crossed the railroad tracks and found a black lady who reluctantly put us up in her COLORED ONLY hotel for the night. We checked in, drank our beer, and then wandered about to investigate the new town before reporting in at Bragg the next day.

Replete in our khaki uniforms, low-quarter shoes, and saucer caps, we proudly made our way to Hay Street, also known as "Combat Alley." This well-known avenue, popular since World War II, had seen countless numbers of "straight leg" recruits come here to make their "cherry run."

As we made our way down the street, we were greeted with the cheerful smiles of high school girls, along with the amusement and contempt of a gaggle of experienced airborne troopers. Soon, catcalls began to ring out and about a dozen young soldiers began to follow us, smashing empty beer bottles at our feet. Finally, we realized the only way out of this was to turn and fight. The eight of us confronted the rowdy hecklers but were unable to find any takers.

Perhaps this somewhat inebriated horde was impressed with our boldness and unity, or maybe it was the sight of our Military Police collar brass. The 82nd Military Police Company had a tough reputation on Fort Bragg; well-earned on Saturday nights dealing with alcohol induced fistfights and a few overturned MP jeeps.

After checking in at Bragg, I was assigned to Company C, First Airborne Battle Group, 187th Infantry for Jump School. Our long days began and ended with being marched back and forth from training to our unit. Unfortunately, I was to break my ankle on my second jump and be forced to repeat my second two weeks (except for ground school).

One memorable event took place when another soldier, Hasty Evans from Alabama, thought he could intimidate me by making me responsible for keeping his foot and wall lockers ready for inspection. I quickly settled the matter with a fight, and he never imposed upon me again. It did cost me an Article 15, however, after I refused to clean up the mess we made on the platoon floor as ordered by a staff sergeant. Hasty and I got along quite well after that.

CPT Michael J. Conrad, who was later to become one of our great military leaders, administered my so-called nonjudicial punishment. In the years to come, I was to meet him again under much more pleasant circumstances before he retired as a major general.

Finally, graduating from Jump School, I received my "cherry wings" and was now ready for my duty assignment.

TOP—GRADUATION FROM USAMPS (MP SCHOOL) AT FORT GORDON, GA

BOTTOM—GRADUATION FROM JUMP SCHOOL (NOTE: I AM STILL WEAR-ING MY MILITARY POLICE COLLAR BRASS)

TOP—READY TO JUMP WITH COMPANY A, 519TH MI BATTALION (I AM THIRD FROM THE LEFT)

BOTTOM —MAKING JUMP WITH CO C, 1ST AIRBORNE BATTLE GROUP, 187th INFANTRY IN 1961

AN MP IN THE AIRBORNE INFANTRY

As part of the 82nd Airborne Division at Fort Bragg and Jump School qualified, the natural transition would have been for me and my MP buddies to be assigned to the 82nd or 18th Military Police Companies. Because these were well over strength, five of the eight of us who had completed jump training after MP school were sent to infantry units.

I was to spend the next couple of years in the infantry as an enlisted man with the 187th. First, I carried the old 3.5-inch Bazooka. Then, as a specialist-4, I became a machine gunner on the old thirty-caliber with an assistant gunner and ammo bearer.

. . .

As Fidel Castro was exporting his revolution and Russia was flexing her Cold War muscles, the call went out for individuals capable of speaking foreign languages. Able to speak fluent German and Hungarian, I applied to the 519th Military Intelligence and was accepted into Company A of this multilingual unit of paratroopers.

Some of the other men were Bosek from Poland, Koreck from the Czech Republic, and Joe Horvath and Steve Baranyi from Hungary. I also met John Rodriguez, who had been brought in with dozens of other Spanish speakers during the time of the Cuban Missile Crisis. John and I would cross paths much later in Vietnam.

John Rodriguez and I became interested in joining the Special Forces and went over to visit the army's Psychological Warfare Center on Smoke Bomb Hill. We had heard there was a war going on in the Southeast Asia country of Vietnam and were curious. We inquired of an NCO who had served a six-month tour over there. "Is it a real shooting war?" we asked.

His answer was clear and blunt. "When you see a machine gun popping up in your face—you'll believe it!"

We left our names to volunteer, but other events quickly took over. John was sent to Miami to work with the Contras who wanted Castro and his communists out. I was to work as a guerrilla under Special Forces guidance against the 82nd Airborne in field training exercises.

On one of these maneuvers, I stayed out a little too long firing my blanks after my SF mentors left the area. I was actually captured by my old infantry company. Hasty Evans, a black soldier from Alabama who always called me "Nicky," was glad to see me. The other guys who remembered me were also happy to be reacquainted and were kind. All of this changed, however, when they turned me over to a military intelligence group from the 101st Airborne Division that specialized in POW interrogations.

I will only say that I was stripped of all my clothing, gassed, tortured, and hanged in a parachute harness from a tree. Then wires from a field phone were attached to my toes and the phone cranked to full force. Their efforts to make me talk did not succeed; however, they all learned some new words that day as I spewed forth every foul expletive I could hurl their way, promising to hunt each of them down and kill them!

Later, my "cooler head" prevailed, and the threats were not carried out, of course. There was a bit of humor in it, too, when some months later, I received TDY orders to Fort Campbell, Kentucky to work with these same individuals. When I arrived at Campbell to report for duty, I was surprised to find an empty office with a lone second lieutenant standing behind a screen. Apparently, they had heard I was coming, and the lieutenant was there to advise me that they didn't want any trouble.

One of the more pleasant experiences I had was to stand in ranks with part of our division on October 12, 1961 and listen to President John F. Kennedy speak. The most memorable part of his speech is quoted below:

> *I want to express my appreciation to the officers and men of the 82nd Airborne for this opportunity to see a group of Americans who do in peacetime what other men do in war, and that is, live hazardously in defense of their country.*

Later, the President went to Smoke Bomb Hill to meet with Brigadier General William P. Yarborough and address the men of the Special Forces. The President remarked to BG Yarborough, "Those are nice. How do you like the Green Beret?"

General Yarborough replied, "They're fine, sir. We've wanted them a long time."

President Kennedy formally recognized the Green Beret as the official headgear of the United States Army Special Forces.

DOMINICAN REPUBLIC: OPERATION POWER PACK

In April of 1965, communist inspired rebels had overrun much of Santo Domingo, the capitol city of the Dominican Republic. People were dying in the streets. President Lyndon Johnson, concerned that the Dominican Republic would become a "second Cuba," ordered part of the 82nd Airborne to be sent by air, and one marine division by sea, to put down the revolt. This intervention was known as Operation Power Pack.

I deployed from Fort Bragg with the 82nd, fully armed and wearing a parachute. We were ready to jump when informed that Pathfinders and Special Forces on the ground with forces loyal to the government had secured the San Isidro Airport. We landed at the airfield and drove the twenty kilometers to the city of Santo Domingo. We made our first contact with the rebels at the Duarte Bridge. When we crossed into the city, we were immediately under fire.

There were about a dozen rebels attempting to keep us from coming into the city with a machine gun and carbines. Their efforts were short-lived, as were their lives, when paratroopers brought up a jeep with a mounted 106mm recoilless rifle or RR.

The 106 had a single-barreled, .50 caliber "spotter rifle" mounted to the tube of the RR to act as a sighting device. Firing a single incendiary round, the spotter creates a cloud of white smoke at the target. Since the ballistics of the RR and the spotter are evenly matched, the round from the RR will hit exactly where the spotter round landed.

In short, all of the rebels who had been firing at us were gone within a moment.

Continuing through the city along the main road, we came under sniper fire from the rooftops, mostly at intersections. I graciously returned fire from my position in the jump seat. Some of the marines were already on the main road behind buildings and seemed amused at how the "newbies" reacted to the incoming. Sadly, we did pass a dead paratrooper, lying near an intersection, shot in the throat.

Part of Santo Domingo was still under government control with some of their soldiers contemplating joining the rebels; however, when they saw us come into town in force, they decided that communism was not for them.

There was fighting street to street for about two-and-a-half weeks. This was usually in late afternoons and evenings when the rebel forces had imbibed sufficiently on the local rum to make themselves feel invincible.

Several days later, American troops were receiving sniper fire from boats on the Ozama River, in particular, a 350-foot freighter named the SS Santo Domingo that had been abandoned to the rebels. A crew from 2nd Battalion, 508th Parachute Infantry Regiment of the 82nd Airborne, brought up a106mm recoilless rifle and blasted the ship. I watched as the ship caught fire and drifted to a sandbar where it ran aground. Some days later, being curious, I swam out to inspect its burned out hull. It was just another day in the life of a soldier.

Our military intelligence unit set up a POW compound to the rear of the Duarte Bridge where we had first entered. With the 82nd MP Company providing security, we were quite safe working 12-hour shifts interrogating detainees.

Each afternoon around 4:00, we would send a jeep to the 18th Airborne Corps Headquarters with the interrogation reports. I volunteered to ride shotgun on these missions, seated in the back of the jeep with my M14 rifle.

One day, while riding in our jeep, SP5 Zdrodowski, known as "Ski," LT Collins, and I suddenly came under sniper fire at one of the intersections. The jeep stalled as bullets hit the ground all around us, throwing up chunks of concrete everywhere. I looked at Ski, whose lips were moving but no sound was coming out. I quickly jumped into the front seat between him and the lieutenant, and with my left foot depressed the starter on the floor, and we chugged safely through the intersection out of the line of fire.

After control had been reestablished, the Dominicans were going after those in their own ranks that had helped stir up the rebel cause. I went in a three-quarter ton truck with a US major, several MPs, and a Dominican army officer to pick up a rather high-ranking local official from his well-appointed home. We brought him out and put him in the back of the truck with us. The major told me to shoot him if he tried to escape. Fortunately, it did not come to that. My plan was to use physical, rather than deadly, force if needed. While I have killed the enemy in combat on numerous occasions, I have never murdered anyone. It was sad enough taking this man away from his family. I can still remember the forlorn look in his eyes.

The Dominicans did not treat their prisoners very well. Sometime later, CPT Parrish, our unit's senior officer on the ground, had been instructed by those higher up to send a Deuce and a Half truck loaded with C rations to a site where the Dominican Army was holding prisoners.

LT Collins and I escorted the truck with SP5 Zdrodowski as the driver. When we arrived, we found about one hundred people, including women and children, crammed into a dozen or so wire cages with no food or water that we could see. The Dominican soldiers, under the direction of an overweight colonel chewing on a cigar and waving a US .45 caliber Thompson submachine gun, were quite aggressive as they approached our jeep and the Deuce and a Half behind us. One of them started to pat me down for cigarettes as I knocked his hand away. At this point, LT Collins told Ski to turn the jeep around and leave.

I said, "Sir, we can't do that. Our mission is to ensure that the prisoners get fed!"

We got out of the jeep, approached the boisterous colonel, and with the help of an interpreter, explained why we were there. Still waving the Thompson, he informed us that we could leave, and he would take care of the prisoners. I stood in front of him with one hand on one of my hand grenades and again reminded him why we had brought the rations.

With much fanfare, he ordered his soldiers to unload the truck, and we watched the prisoners eat at least one meal. Before departing, I shared a cigarette with the soldier who first tried to shake me down.

A NEW OFFICER JOINS THE SPECIAL FORCES

While on deployment to the Dominican Republic for several months, I received orders to report back to Bragg and appear before the OCS board (Officer Candidate School). I departed the DR on a C-130 aircraft but, unfortunately, my flight was mixed with sadness as I was to share it with another soldier, slain by a fellow brother-in-arms over a woman. I remember his body bag on the tailgate packed in ice, and as it melted, reddish fluid drained out onto the ramp.

Showing up for my OCS board, following a successful combat operation, was a piece of cake. Lean, tanned, and confident, the three field grade officers who held my future in their hands seemed more interested in my deployment to the DR and what I had been through than my personal traits and whether I had what it took to be a commissioned officer.

In September of 1965, I reported to Fort Benning, Georgia for Officer Candidate School, wearing my bloused boots befitting my status as an airborne soldier. The next six months were quite eventful, and I can best explain my experiences as being tested for my capacity to endure harassment while being trained to lead soldiers in combat as an officer.

The course included much physical conditioning as well as training in the matter of infantry weapons and tactics. For the first nine weeks, the tactical officers used both intensity and humor to get us to quit. The phrase, "You don't belong here!" was often heard.

For some reason, perhaps because I was there from Fort Bragg, some of the cadre thought I was already SF qualified as a "Sneaky Pete." They would make me low crawl through the dining hall, attempting to "sneak" past them to get my meal. Then I was made to consume it while sitting erect on the first four inches of my dining room chair. A friend, Thomas Humphus, also from Bragg, had served in the Special Forces and had endured a similar fate.

On March 18, 1966, the 52nd OCS Company graduated less than fifty percent of the officer candidates that started during the previous six months. Pinning on our "butter bars," we set out as brand-new second lieutenants in the United States Army to change the world.

Anticipating my eventual service in Vietnam, I knew that it was customary for a new second lieutenant to be assigned to a unit to get his feet wet before being deployed to a war zone.

"What better place than the Special Forces!" I thought.

. . .

I had put on my dream sheet a desire to join the Special Forces. Urged on by my older brother, Laszlo, who was at that time a Washington, DC policeman, and himself with the Special Forces in the Army Reserve, I requested to be assigned to the 10th Special Forces in Bad Tolz, Germany. The 10th SF had an in-country SF qualification training program and a mission that involved countering communism in Europe which, as a Hungarian refugee, appealed to me immensely.

Although much of the army's focus was shifting to Vietnam to counter the guerrilla war there, the 10th SF retained their mission of leading organized guerrilla operations in Europe. After receiving my orders for the 10th Special Forces, I went home to Cleveland for a short leave.

One interesting treat was that on my flight from Atlanta to Washington, DC, I got to ride on the same airplane as Senator Bobby

Kennedy, the President's younger brother. I still remember his wife, Ethel, smile as they walked with their entourage of kids. I wished I had asked for his autograph as did a number of the passengers.

After my leave, I flew to Germany to begin my Special Forces training. After I arrived, I took a train to Bad Tolz, dressed in my Class A uniform, where I encountered some unruly men at the train station. The rowdies, undoubtedly off duty soldiers dressed in their civilian clothes, thought it would be easy to intimidate a second lieutenant wearing his "butter bars." Taking off my green uniform jacket, I informed them that if they "wanted some," I would be happy to oblige. Finding no takers among the group, I watched as they wandered off, quite subdued.

Arriving at the 10th Special Forces group headquarters, I was greeted by a major who was the adjutant. He wasted no time in informing me that, as a brand-new second lieutenant and not Special Forces qualified, I had to speak with Colonel Cavanaugh, the group commander, to determine if I could stay or if I had to be reassigned to another unit.

During the interview, the colonel was kind but tough as he looked over my personnel file. He informed me that there were very few second lieutenants in the group, but the ones he had were very good. I informed him that I could learn anything I needed to accomplish the mission. He informed me that he didn't have the time to teach me. Slightly chagrined, I told him that I was fluent in both Hungarian and German. Looking at me he said, "We can certainly use your languages. I will give you sixty days to prove yourself," and assigned me to B Company, under the command of then MAJ Martin Beck, a singularly tough officer who welcomed me with open arms.

The 10th was a highly elite unit that trained constantly. Moreover, they conducted real-world missions in various European nations and had a good reputation. As there was an ORTT currently in progress, unique to the 10th's ongoing mission, I had to make a parachute jump the next day. In order to participate, I was required to be given jump refresher training by MAJ Beck. This consisted of me performing a PLF by jumping off a three-foot log, which I did successfully. MAJ Beck smiled and called it "good."

Special Forces is all about flexibility and innovation. As the new guy, I was given the honor of carrying the generator that would provide the power for our shortwave radio by which we communicated in Morse code. The extra twenty pounds did not bother me much, and we made a successful, low-level night insertion jumping from a C-47 aircraft.

LT Douglas Coulter, the honor graduate of his OCS class, and I were given the mission to walk twenty-six miles, with some enlisted men from the 8th Infantry who were our guerrillas, and were to make an extraction of a "High Value Asset." We accomplished our mission, and all others, during the two-week exercise. Upon returning and being relatively unknown in the group, I was sent out in civilian clothes to infiltrate the ORT of A Company. I approached the perimeter speaking only Hungarian and was interrogated, processed, and eventually released.

After that, I was sent to a Bad Wiessee for water training, Hohenfels for weapons and demolitions, and to Lenggries for communications. I became proficient enough to send and receive twenty words per minute in Morse code.

After the successful completion of my training, and there being a shortage of captains, LTC Beck made me commander of SF Detachment A-25 with the mission, in the event of hostilities, to jump into Hungary, organize a guerrilla army, and kill the enemy. While we were never deployed, the mission suited us well. This was also true for the other two native-born Hungarians in our team, particularly our team sergeant, Victor Kreisman, a Hungarian Jew. Kreisman had emigrated to Israel and fought with Irgun, a Jewish underground organization, and Tibor Bierbaum against the communists during the Hungarian Revolution in 1956.

In late summer of 1966, our team was successfully tested in all phases of SF missions. We jumped in from low-level on the continent, moved and communicated by setting up directional antennas using shortwave radios, and made every objective assigned over an extended operation.

Upon our return, there was some time spent in garrison followed by a visit from an Austrian general who was there to coordinate military matters of interest to both our nations. The general inquired if there were any Hungarian SF in the 10th Group. Perhaps this was because of the Hungarians strong anti-communist stand and because his mother was Hungarian. The general was informed that there was, and they mentioned me as an example. I was assigned as the general's *aide-de-camp* during his weeklong stay.

Soon after, I met COL Cavanaugh in passing and I asked him how my transition was going. His short, cheerful response was, "You are one of us, Hun!"

Some months later, with a new designation of MOS 31542, Special Forces Qualified Infantry Officer, I was assigned to the 5th Special Forces Group in Vietnam. My transition was complete, but the heavy lifting was yet to come! LTC Beck also went to Vietnam, but sadly, lost his life as a hero helping his troops when their helicopter was shot down. We lost a great man on that sad day.

OPENING CAMP CHI LINH

In October of 1966, I was assigned to detachment A-342 in Dong Xoai, Vietnam, located about fifty-five miles north of Saigon. The camp commander was CPT Charles Steinmetz, who had also served in the 10th Group in Germany. We bonded instantly. CPT Steinmetz sent me out on numerous operations with guaranteed enemy contact to break in this new second lieutenant.

In early November of 1966, the reins of our A detachment command passed from CPT Steinmetz to CPT Ambrose Brennan. I was his executive officer.

Our general AO (Area of Operations) was War Zone D which was roughly south and east of Dong Xoai, consisting of many square miles of thick, almost impenetrable, three-canopy jungle. The NVA (North Vietnamese Army) and the VC (Viet Cong) had heavily infiltrated the area making it a convenient staging point for enemy operations in South Vietnam.

At the same time, SF detachment A-333 was under construction at Chí Linh under the command of CPT Doyle E. Smith. A MIKE Force out of Nha Trang (5th Special Forces HQ) was sent in to secure the campsite on the west side of the Song Be River. A MIKE Force (Mobile Assault Team) consists of specially trained indigenous soldiers under SF leadership, used primarily for special and, typically, dangerous operations.

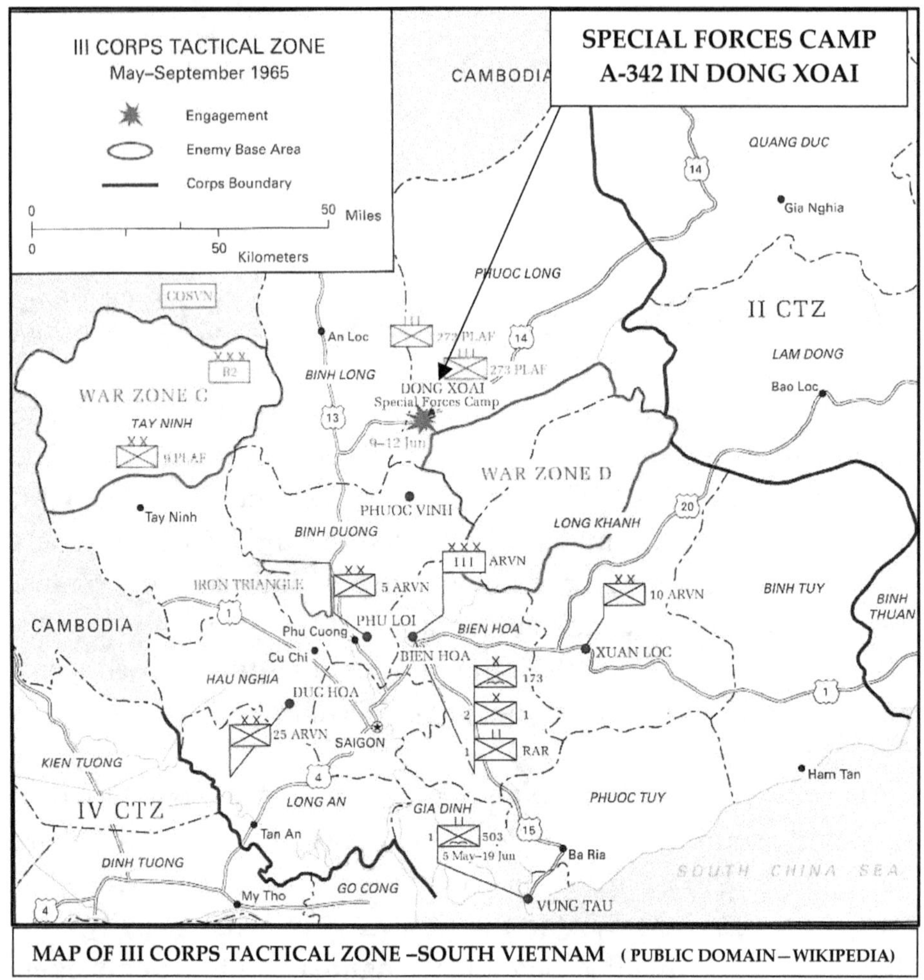

MAP OF III CORPS TACTICAL ZONE –SOUTH VIETNAM (PUBLIC DOMAIN—WIKIPEDIA)

SFC Ed O'Neal, SGT Phillip Crowell, Vietnamese SF CPT Chu, and I, along with two companies of Cambodian strikers, went in by helicopter, landing by a downed bridge on Hwy 14 just east of the SB River. Our helicopters came in hot with machine guns blazing, as they normally did when deep in enemy territory.

Arriving at our LZ (Landing Zone), I quickly disembarked the chopper by jumping out about five feet off the ground. The Huey pilot, departing as hot as he had come in, veered sharply up and away. When the Huey was about twenty yards off the ground, a three-foot section of the 7.62mm ammunition belt tore loose from the

M-60 machine gun mounted in the doorway, striking me on the head and knocking me unconscious.

I'm not exactly sure what happened but, sometimes in the heat of battle, the door gunner might jerk his weapon, or the chopper pilot might make an erratic turn, causing the belt of ammunition in the machine gun to break off. The cloth bush hats that the SF wore on these operations afforded little protection against a flying bandolier of heavy brass and lead.

I had no actual memory of this event until retired SGM Ed O'Neal[1] contacted me about thirty years later in the States. I rode my Harley down to North Carolina to visit him where he lived on a large farm with his wife, Mary, whom he met on his first tour in Vietnam. She had worked there for the State Department in Saigon in the early sixties.

After we talked, it all came back to me. I then remembered lying on the ground bleeding and him shouting, "Wake up, LT!" as he threw water in my face. I also recalled that the stray belt of ammo did not go to waste, by the way. I took it with me on our recon mission and later fired it at the enemy.

SFC Ed O'Neal and CPT Chu took one company of strikers and patrolled north of the highway, east of the Song Be River. SGT Crowell and I took the other and headed south toward Phuoc Vinh, also east of the river.

The strikers, known as CIDG (Civilian Irregular Defense Group), were indigenous soldiers trained and led by the Special Forces, primarily made up of local civilians (ours were Cambodians) displaced by the communists. Our mission was to recon an area reported to have large concentrations of enemy forces. This was partly for the

---

[1] *About seven years ago, I went back to Memorial Hospital in Rockingham, NC as Ed lay in hospice care and did my best to comfort his wife, Mary, who stayed with him. Captain Brennan was also there before Ed's passing. Ed was a very brave man.*

benefit of the 1st Infantry Division who was planning an operation there and needed additional intelligence.

On that first day, miles from any town or village, we made our initial contact about seven clicks out. We knew we were close to a camp when we discovered numerous well-worn trails marked with tire tracks from various types of vehicles, including bicycles.

As we neared a large tear-shaped LZ, our Cambodian strikers, under the leadership of an aspiring Vietnamese lieutenant, stopped and refused to go any farther. The lieutenant was known to have fought on the side of the enemy in the past. He understood that the area was not a particularly healthy place to be, that is, unless you were wearing the khaki uniform and pith helmet of the North Vietnamese Army.

Our Cambodians were childlike in many respects and very superstitious. They were afraid to leave their dead behind for religious reasons. Believing in luck and karma, they would sometimes place the Buddhas from their gold-chained necklaces in their mouths and chant as they went into battle.

SGT Crowell and I continued with our mission, accompanied by only five Cambodian strikers that had been ordered to go with us. A little over a mile farther south, we soon located the enemy complex constructed of several acres of bunkers and fighting positions and a tin-covered, barracks-sized building loaded with stored rice.

I came upon a strange looking pit about thirty feet in circumference and decided to examine it more closely by walking on it. I was looking into the hole in the middle, trying to figure out what it was, when I noticed that our Cambodians seemed puzzled by my actions. Finally, one of them bluntly shouted, *"S—t!"* Their inquisitive Special Forces lieutenant had stumbled upon the community latrine. Combat is not without its lighter moments.

One of the many brave, and often unsung, heroes in the Vietnam War was the FAC (Forward Air Controller) who flew above the battlefields in a Cessna L-19/O-1 Bird Dog, a single-prop, light observation plane.

Often flying his Bird Dog within fifty feet of the treetops, he would communicate with ground troops in need of assistance, diligently conducting reconnaissance to assess their plight below. Then, with accurate coordinates, the daring FAC would request the needed fire support to respond by aircraft or artillery. Marking the enemy targets with white phosphorus rockets, he would correct and adjust their fire by direct visual observation.

We radioed our discovery of the enemy camp to the FAC flying above us who, in turn, notified the artillery in Phuoc Vinh. Their response was for us to get out of there so they could "pound it" with delayed fuse rounds (used in thick-canopied jungle) to uproot the enemies' digs. We were most happy to comply!

The last thing our FAC said to me was, "You'd better get out of there, DX5 (my call sign as the A Team XO at Dong Xoai). I see a couple hundred of them coming after you!" He then fired his white phosphorus rockets at them and stated, "By the way, I am climbing to three thousand feet!" indicating that he wanted to be well out of range of any "flak" from the approaching enemy and the artillery rounds soon to be coming to "Charlie" from Phuoc Vinh.

I was the last one out from our seven-man recon team. I quickly threw my last grenade and as I turned to leave, my tiger suit seemed to be snagged on something. As I glanced back to see what it was, there stood a North Vietnamese soldier holding on to my sleeve, attempting to make me his prisoner. Earlier, I had rolled my sleeves down after coming into contact with some vicious fire ants while searching the NVA camp.

I finally broke away from the little guy holding my arm, who appeared more shaken than I was. One of our Cambodian strikers told me later that this fellow was only obeying orders from his superiors to "catch one of them alive!" His AK rifle lay on the ground next to him, so I did not consider killing him. My immediate concern was to get out of there because I could clearly hear the chatter of his associates coming our way from the nearby jungle. The killing time would come later.

As I ran to leave, I missed the turn to the path we had taken earlier to the large LZ adjacent to the NVA base camp. [2]SGT Crowell shouted back, "This way, LT!" I thanked God for sergeants that day!

Now on the right track, and being quite physically fit, I easily passed the five, short-legged Cambodians of our recon unit who were making their getaway. It suddenly struck me, as their trainer and leader, that it might not appear dignified to be running ahead of them from danger.

The courageous FAC above us had left to refuel, so we were on our own. We hurried to reunite with the remainder of our CIDG irregulars, who we hoped were still waiting for us several clicks down the path with their golden Buddhas in their mouths, chanting for good karma.

I abruptly stopped and asked one of the CIDG for the PRC-25 radio to call for more artillery and available air support to kill "Charlie" and his cohorts from the north before they could kill us. With the shrugging of shoulders, I was told in Vietnamese or Cambodian, I don't remember which, that our only PRC-25 had been dropped by the CIDG carrying it during our hasty retreat. Having been bailed out by SGT Crowell earlier, I turned to him and said, "Phil, get the radio!"

As he started back toward the pursuing enemy, who were now chattering even louder and closer, I realized that this was not right and ran ahead of him, half dragging the CIDG irregular who had been guilty of losing the radio.

We finally located it on the ground about fifty yards back on the trail just as one of the Cambodian irregulars came along beside me carrying an M79 grenade launcher. After a quick retrieval of our prized possession, it was once again time to leave, particularly since we were on the edge of the large LZ with very little cover.

---

[2] *SGT Phillip E. Crowell, retired, currently resides in Florida. We communicate regularly in a manner only possible by those who have shared the crucible of war.*

The chatter of the enemy was getting much too close, and we were receiving some "incoming" from the tree line about 75 yards out. It was time to break contact with them, but first, to "get some" before departing.

I took the M79 from the striker next to me and zeroed in on the tree line where the bushes showed some movement. I was experienced firing the old M20 (3.5 inch) bazooka in training with the 1st Airborne Battle Group of the 187th Infantry at Fort Bragg, making the conversion to the M79 fairly easy.

Having a relatively free line of fire, I shot the M79 toward the enemy three times. The first round impacted long and the second one short. This established a bracket around the target, allowing me to place the final round with deadly accuracy. As I fired one more time, the HE (high explosive) round landed just as four or five NVA soldiers, with AK and SKS rifles at the ready, stepped proudly out of the heavy jungle into the tall grass.

We heard them scream and watched them fall, helmets flying like Frisbees, as they were instantly blown up in a haze of gray smoke. Departing, I turned one last time to witness their throes of death in the smoking elephant grass.

...

That evening, we had pulled back to our main unit of nervous CIDG strikers and spent the night there, listening while the artillery from Phuoc Vinh pounded the enemy camp with 175mm shells.

The following day, SFC O'Neal and CPT Chu, along with their company of CIDG, joined us, and together, we went back into the camp two companies strong (about 200 men). I walked in our lone M60 machine gun and found the ground littered with bloodied bandages, evidence of the previous night's artillery pounding. The foul stench of death was everywhere. Add to this the permeating odor of "nuoc mam," a fermented fish sauce, and you have a good indication that enemy soldiers are nearby.

Again, as we made contact with the enemy, our strikers quickly got on line and dropped to the ground. Artillery support was requested from Chi Linh, and before long, 105mm howitzer shells began raining down upon the enemy in front of us. Then, for whatever reason, a short round landed only twenty feet from me, exploding about five-hundred feet closer than intended.

Everything suddenly turned "blue" from the concussion, and to this day, I'm not sure if it was my fault (a second lieutenant with a map) or the Vietnamese crew shooting out of a new camp in a strange area for the first time. Fortunately, Ed O'Neal immediately called for a cease-fire so that no further self-imposed damage could be inflicted. Some days we were our own worst enemies!

Ed O'Neal had positioned himself next to me and the radio, probably to ensure that we wouldn't have a repeat of the short round incident. Then, to Ed's amusement, he said, "Look behind you, LT!" Sure enough, about a dozen or so of our strikers were no longer in place but were directly behind me in a straight line as I fired the M60 machine gun.

I was told that the CIDG strikers considered me lucky, inspiring them to hunker down on either side of me when the bullets were flying. I later came to believe that rather than it being my luck, the strikers were mostly obeying orders from their officers. My life was to be preserved at all costs as I was their lifeline for radio communications, resupply, and the evacuation of their wounded.

...

Later, before leaving, we swept the area and then headed back north to Hwy 14 to hang out by the bridge at Chi Linh to help with security. I couldn't resist taking a swim across the shallow Song Be River to get into the camp, much to the surprise of the SF and engineers. I had to tease them about their perimeter security needing some work!

Actually, the CIDG on guard duty clearly saw me coming in with no shirt, wet tiger suit pants, and carrying my M16, so they knew I was an American, either from the MIKE Force or Dong Xoai. I did, however, get a few "crazy American" looks from the Cambodian guards.

Later extracted by chopper, we returned to our A Team at Dong Xoai where I found a major general from the 1st Infantry Division waiting to speak with me. Having just arrived by chopper himself, he seemed quite sleepy, judging by his yawning. I quickly gave him a debriefing before cleaning up, suspecting that our brave FAC had advised him of our earlier adventures. Though I mentioned the FAC's great support to the sleepy general, I regret to this day that I did not put him in for an award for his heroism.

TOP—BRIDGE OVER THE SONG BE RIVER AT CHI LINH
BELOW—DEEP IN THE BUSH BEFORE A MAJOR BATTLE—JANUARY 1967 AT CHI LINH

DOWNED BRIDGE ON THE SONG BE RIVER AT CHI LINH

CAMP DONG XOAI

The Vietnamese village of Dong Xoai (DX for short), and SF detachment camp A-342 were located in Phuoc Long Province alongside Hwy 14. In June of 1965, this was the scene of a horrific battle where approximately 1,500 Viet Cong overran the camp. When it was all over, there were 20 Americans killed or wounded with 13 missing, along with 416 Vietnamese dead, 174 wounded and 233 missing. This confirmed that DX was a serious place where one had to be strong and lucky to survive.

AERIALVIEW OF DONG XOAI IN JUNE 1965. AUTHOR—JACK WATERS (PUBLIC DOMAIN—WIKIPEDIA)

In early 1967, the US efforts to win the war were increasing, and new American units were being inserted. The Special Forces footprint was also expanding, e.g., Chi Linh, and later, Bunard.

In DX, there were continuous operations conducted by two of our five companies of CIDG irregulars led by at least one LLDB (Vietnamese SF) officer. As was our custom, two US SF would accompany each CIDG company out on combat operations lasting around five days. We normally had one or two of these companies out who never failed to make contact with the enemy. This made our camp relatively safe from being overrun as it had been in 1965. Of course, there were frequent probes and mortar attacks that had to be repelled. Large VC and NVA units often moved in near proximity to our camp as they amassed forces for their offensives.

Since we had two officers on the SF team, CPT Brennan and I would alternate going out, thus, we were seldom in camp together. Everyone went on combat operations, but we still would have seven or eight SF guys in camp to defend against attacks on the camp itself, which occurred with regularity. As the team XO, my position was in the tower where there were a couple of 30 caliber machine guns mounted.

I remember Captain Steinmetz telling me to be careful during night probes on the camp as I was blasting away with the 30 caliber. He said, "They will blow you out of there with an RPG if they can home in on you." I then changed to shorter bursts.

After returning from our January excursion in Chi Linh, our A detachment at Dong Xoai continued its mission of "reconnaissance-in-force" in their vast AO, under the direction of the Special Forces B Team in Song Be, commanded by LTC Jacques W. Bernier, and the C Team under LTC Thomas M. Huddleston in Bien Hoa.

CPT Brennan and SFC Ed O'Neal returned to the Chi Linh region in February of '67, making heavy enemy contact and suffering casualties. Requesting a fire mission, the Air Force sent "Spooky" (also known as Puff the Magic Dragon), a specially modified, fixed-wing, World War II, C-47 aircraft (redesignated AC-47) mounted with a system of three GE rotary miniguns (each having six barrels). "Puff" was capable of laying down a barrage of 7.62mm bullets every square foot in a swath the width of a football field. With the AC-47 capable of flying over the enemy at a speed of 120 knots, the effects of its guns were devastating.

I remember watching from our A Team camp in DX and seeing Puff's guns pounding the area well into the night. We could hear the NVA chattering and singing on the radio, ostensibly to block our communications or just to simply unnerve us. Either way, Puff did not do them any favors with her miniguns spewing red phosphorus tracer rounds from above, streaking the sky like a fireworks display and shredding the trees and everything else that happened to be in its path.

There were a couple of CIDG strikers from DX wounded in the fray who were treated with IV morphine and evacuated by chopper the following morning. CPT Brennan later visited one of these men at the CIDG hospital in Bien Hoa.

A little-known battle took place in March of '67, near the Cambodian border, that cost two brave SF soldiers their lives. A strike force from A Team (A-341) out of Bu Dop had been ambushed, forcing them to leave a number of bodies behind. A Mobile Strike Force from B Team 36 MSFC, led by CPT Jack T. Stewart and SSG Roger C. Hallberg, was called upon to retrieve the bodies. However, security for the mission had been compromised and two battalions of the VC 9th Division—between 500 and 700 men, were waiting there for them.

We were alerted at Dong Xoai and advised to get a strike force ready to go bail them out, but we were never committed. Stewart and Hallberg were never seen or heard from again. How sad! I knew Roger Hallberg—a nice, mild-mannered guy.

These things did not fail to go unnoticed by the 1st Infantry Division, and after our A Team departed to Bunard, Operation Billings was launched later that year, in June, against elements of the 271 VC Regiment. This happened to be near the place southeast of Chi Linh at the large tear-shaped LZ where SGT Crowell and I, along with our five Cambodian CIDG from our recon platoon, began making life uncomfortable for the NVA earlier in January. Heavy fighting ensued, but Operation Billings was considered a success with 347 of the enemy killed compared to 57 American losses.

...

There was a substantial interest in the welfare of the Special Forces at Phuoc Vinh by the 1st Infantry Division commanders, MG John H. Hay, and one of his brigade commanders, COL Sidney B. Berry Jr. Regularly launching battalion-sized operations in War Zone D and beyond, they regarded the SF A Team camps a perpetual source of combat intelligence. These two enlightened commanders saw the SF as a highly vulnerable human resource to be nourished and protected.

MG Hay and COL Berry, great leaders of the "Big Red One," did their best to keep us SF guys alive and well. They would often send liaison teams of artillery officers to our camps to ensure that we had all the support we needed.

COL Berry would send Christmas cards and notes to show that he respected us and our mission and would sometimes make visits himself. In a way, we were their eyes and ears as large VC and NVA units regularly moved close to the A Camps. Undoubtedly, that is one of the reasons we were there.

Air America would fly in rice, etc., for the indigenous troops, but except for C-Rations, we had to make our own periodic runs for supplies because the A Teams were not on any regular food chain. Often, COL Berry would send OH-13 type helicopters to our camp, and one of us would fly back to Phuoc Vinh in the right seat for a food run.

On one of these flights to Phuoc Vinh, at about one thousand feet, I looked out the right door below and there was a line, several hundred yards long, of NVA soldiers carrying their normal weapons, including several 82mm mortars in broad daylight. Just to make sure they were not our allies, we chatted with Phuoc Vinh to confirm that they were indeed enemy soldiers. The pilot then called for 175mm artillery support. We went up to about 5,000 feet, as I recall, and watched as some of the rounds sailed in to find their mark. The 175mm is a large shell but can be a bit erratic due to the lack of rifling. The enemy quickly scrambled after spotting us, but I am certain a substantial number were killed as they had no cover or bunkers to jump into.

...

From late in 1966 to early '67, we conducted numerous patrols from Dong Xoai to Bunard, typically walking the 17 kilometers up Hwy 14 to the northeast with a company of 100 CIDG, led by one LLDB and two American SF A Team members. Though approximately 2,500 Vietnamese civilians were living in the area, mostly underground, the area was designated a "free-fire zone" for US forces. This meant that anything on the ground was considered hostile and could be engaged.

This was one of the fallacies of Vietnam; the civilians living there had no control over who lorded over them and could easily be targeted by the VC/NVA or the US and South Vietnamese forces. Such isolated areas abounded in the countryside and were utilized by the Viet Cong as bases for recruiting and food supply. Their growing rice fields and vegetable gardens could be easily seen from the air.

A Camps were typically built in these areas as the SF sought to wrest the populace away from the communist side. Such was eventually to be the case once we built the camp at Bunard where the over 2,500 civilians came out from where they had been living underground in fear, their skin washed out and pale from the lack of sunlight.

Just before Christmas in 1966, CPT Chu, SGT Crowell, SGT Browder, and I went there by foot from DX with a company of our

Cambodian irregulars. There we made contact with a reinforced platoon of Viet Cong, armed with AK-47s, 60mm mortars, and light machine guns. The engagement continued for about 15 minutes as the VC began firing their mortars.

At this point, CPT Chu ordered the CIDG to engage the enemy, which turned out to be a brilliant move. As we attacked forward firing our weapons, this resulted in us running clear of the mortar's impact area. There was no cover except for some light vegetation, which would have resulted in a lot of carnage for us.

The VC were completely surprised by our bold move and retreated post haste, leaving a dozen mortar rounds, as well as the mortar sighting device, and two of their dead. Judging by the blood trails, they had taken several wounded with them.

Our damage was five CIDG strikers with mortar shrapnel wounds, none of which were life threatening. We contacted our A Team at DX and Captains Brennan and Steinmetz, who were still in transition as commanders, were able to get choppers in the air to come and get us.

We carried our wounded to an improvised LZ on a hillside, sweating profusely from the fight and the humidity and blazing afternoon sun. As the choppers landed, red clay dust blew over us, covering our sweat-soaked faces and uniforms all bloodied from carrying the heavy wounded. Twisting my ankle as I guided the choppers in, I was the last to board the trail helicopter.

I remember the pilot looking at me from his lift in the left front seat and smiling, shaking his head. Chopper pilots see a lot and can still laugh about it. I think it was on that day I decided to become one.

Upon returning, I wrote recommendations for valor awards for Jimmy Browder and Phil Crowell that they later received. My reward was to come later when LT Nguyen Cong Trieu, our A Team Vietnamese XO, himself a true hero, used that term in regards to me. I guess he and another hero, CPT Chu, had talked.

In early February of '67, CPT Brennan took a company of CIDG up to Bunard, along with our newly assigned junior medic, SGT Thomas G. Gallant, who, quite befittingly, lived up to his name and was a gallant fighter. Short, stocky, and powerfully built, he had no difficulty dealing with a rucksack, multiple hand grenades (both fragmentation and white phosphorus), and 500 rounds of M16 ammunition we carried in a BAR (Browning Automatic Rifle) cartridge belt on combat operations. Unfortunately, on the second day of the operation, Gallant was shot in the ankle and had to be evacuated by air.

Since all A Teams are required to have an officer on site at all times, 1LT James E. Wilde, the A Team XO at Xom Cat (A-312), was flown in to DX to take command since I had been ordered to Bunard to replace SGT Gallant. The camp at Xom Cat was to close a few months later, and Jim Wilde was to eventually become the XO at Dong Xoai under CPT O'Malley.

Despite his Irish surname, O'Malley was part Filipino, often joking that if things became too hot and the camp was overrun, he would shed his uniform and squat "Vietnamese style," and welcome his liberators in the Vietnamese language. O'Malley, and many of the SF guys, had studied Vietnamese at the US Army Language School in Monterey, California.

LTC Jacques W. Bernier, the B Team commander at Song Be, sent a helicopter to take me to Bunard. When I arrived, there was some sporadic fighting on the ground, so my insertion was delayed for a short time. The pilot jokingly said, "You really didn't want to go down there anyway." I responded, "I would not want to be anywhere else unless you could fly me to Australia for R&R."

After being finally dropped off, CPT Brennan remarked with humor, "You bailed me out again!"

There was much work to be done at Bunard because the day before, ten of our CIDG had been killed on an old dirt road that the VC and NVA used for transport and resupply. Our indigenous troops had to withdraw, leaving the bodies of their comrades strewn upon the ground. Now it was time to retrieve them and deliver some retribution.

Going in, we spread out on both sides of the road until we came upon the bodies of our fallen dead who pitifully lay in various grotesque postures. Although already bloated due to the overnight heat and humidity, the corpses had been spared the indignity of mutilation by the VC. Only their weapons, ammunition, and grenades had been removed.

Using long ropes, we cautiously gave each body several hard tugs from about thirty feet away to ensure that no booby traps had been planted. None were found. The bodies had been left unmolested for a good reason!

Under Buddhist religion and culture, it is vitally important to recover the dead and provide a respectful funeral that involves coffins covered with colorful crepe paper and candles. Then would come the weeping and wailing by the widows as the soldier's remains were cremated. For this reason, the NVA lay in ambush, knowing we would be back to retrieve the bodies. Besides, they certainly were not willing to give up one of their home bases to a couple of SF guys and a bunch of CIDG irregulars who had no designated air support and were out of range of any friendly artillery.

It was at this point that the North Vietnamese decided to make themselves known when several of the enemy stepped out on the dirt road wearing tiger suit uniforms similar to ours. Our interpreter, a nice young Cambodian named Kim Man Mott, attempted to fool them by telling them we were also VC. This ruse failed utterly when orders to "attack!" were shouted out by the NVA's Chinese advisors. Bugles suddenly blared above the enemy's high-pitched chatter as we heard the familiar crack of their AK and SKS rifles, mingled with short, steady bursts of machine gun fire.

Our recon platoon, now in direct contact, returned fire and pulled back to our main body under heavy pressure. With the smell of rotting bodies and cordite heavy in the air, it might have been just another firefight. Unfortunately, or perhaps not, our HT10 handheld radios picked up the enemy radio conversations, indicating we were engaged with a much larger unit than we originally thought. Panic immediately ensued and most of our CIDG troops broke and ran, trampling the bodies of their decomposing comrades from the previous fight who still littered the dirt road.

Somehow, CPT Brennan was able to contact an FAC, flying an L-19, who came to our aid. It was interesting to watch our brave, but very determined, A Team leader, with his short-cropped red hair, as he had lost his bush hat trying to keep our Cambodian CIDG strikers from running away. He held one striker under each arm while talking to the FAC on the radio.

I was about ten yards ahead of him with some cover, engaging the enemy with my M16 as the main body of NVA was still about 75 yards away. I fired five—twenty-round magazines at them as they fled into the bushes to hide.

Once all our troops withdrew, save the recon platoon who were on line with me, it became a free-fire zone to the front if one saw movement. CPT Brennan told me to hold my position, which I did while engaging the enemy. However, my thought process was to grab him and "get out of Dodge" if we were about to be overrun. That is, until two jets from the navy suddenly showed up, diverted from another mission by our brave FAC who literally circled above us as our lifeline.

After a brief conversation with the aircraft, we marked our lonely position with smoke as the jets came in low-level along the road over the massed NVA unit in the attack. Hundreds of CBU (Cluster Bomb Unit) "bomblets," about the size and shape of large pineapples, came out from containers under their wings and exploded among the enemy who were unable to escape because much of the terrain was only sparse vegetation. After several runs, the jets flew over us and grateful salutes were exchanged. Our CIDG troops, witnessing the valiant rescue by our jets, returned to the fold.

Rightly or wrongly, enemy body count received a great deal of importance in those days, and the FAC asked us for a number. CPT

Brennan, a man of great integrity, who never fudged anything, asked me to take a small element from the recon unit and check the battle area.

The first group of dead enemy soldiers, dressed in tan uniforms and badly shredded, were about fifty yards from our position. I could immediately count 22 smoldering carcasses with their weapons blown to pieces. I could see one of the nearby trees strewn with their intestines.

Several from the recon platoon went toward a small clearing where they reported another dozen fallen NVA. In all, I think I reported 28 of the enemy KIA to the good captain, who gave me the dubious look of a West Point graduate. He did report the number to the FAC who was still circling the area, and who probably had drawn his own conclusions regarding the virtual disappearance of what was at least a company-sized NVA unit. I, on the other hand, could have stayed counting bodies downrange longer had it not been for the unexploded CBU burning in the grass and the haunting moans of dying VC and NVA in the near distance.

After the body count recon, we gathered our group, leaving the smoldering NVA bodies to the fate of the jungle. We then returned to our company where our CIDG had already placed our extremely malodorous dead from the day before in ponchos. Bamboo was cut and poles were attached to carry our ten fallen comrades back to DX through the jungle to Hwy 14. There we would meet our lone Deuce and a Half truck and platoon of CIDG who would return them back to camp.

Darkness comes early along the equator, and it was now late afternoon. CPT Brennan wanted to get to the highway that night and back to DX. I objected but was overruled. Later, as the evening shadows set in about 6:00 o'clock, we began making less progress as the dense jungle became more and more difficult to navigate. Carrying our decomposing dead caused several of the men to get sick and vomit. I approached CPT Chu and recommended that we stop for the night. I could see his knowing smile in the nautical twilight, and he gave the order.

Unlike a typical infantry unit, we did not "dig in." We knew we were quite alone in the dark, and it would be unlikely that we would reencounter the enemy, who at this point, were dealing with their own tragedy on a much larger scale.

After realizing what happened, CPT Brennan gave me a very brief lecture about countermanding his orders as we set up our hammocks for a good night's sleep. I responded with silence, except for a courteous, "Good night, sir!"

This was not the first or the last time I did not follow instructions, even though I had, and still have, great respect and admiration for this fine man and exceptional leader. An officer's insignia of rank is actually a symbol of servitude[3] to the soldiers he leads. Accordingly, one sometimes takes great personal risk when he speaks "truth to power," particularly when soldier welfare is in the decision-making equation. CPT Brennan understood that and lived by that motto! We are close friends to this very day.

The CIDG temporarily buried their dead in shallow graves that night to mask the smell. The next day, they were carried back to the highway and driven the five kilometers back home to DX for a proper Buddhist ceremony and cremation.

---

[3] *And whosoever will be chief among you, let him be your servant: Matthew 20:27 (KJV)*

TOP: DONG XOAI SPECIAL FORCES CAMP– (COURTESY OF PHIL CROWELL)
BELOW: DONG XOAI—SF CAMP AND TOWN OF DONG XOAI IN THE NORTHEAST C. 1967

**TOP—CAMBODIAN LADY WHO COOKED FOR OUR A TEAM AT DX
BELOW—CAMBODIAN STRIKERS OF OUR RECON PLATOON AT DONG XOAI SF CAMP**

TOP—OUR A TEAM SHOWER AT DX SF CAMP
BOTTOM—COMMAND BUNKER AT DONG XOAI SF CAMP—1966

TOP—VIEW OF DONG XOAI SF CAMP
BOTTOM—VILLAGE OF DONG XOAI AND OUR SPECIAL FORCES CAMP VISIBLE TO THE SOUTHEAST

CHILDREN OF DONG XOAI

TOP—MORE CHILDREN FROM DONG XOAI
BOTTOM—WIFE OF ONE OF OUR CIDGE TROOPS INSIDE DX SF CAMP

TOP—KIM CHU, OUR RECON PLATOON LEADER AT DONG XOAI
BOTTOM—OUR MEDICAL CLINIC A-TEAM DONG XOAI SF CAMP

TOP—CAMP DONG XOAI SIGN—SPECIAL FORCES A-CAMP DONG XOAI
(COURTESY OF PHIL CROWELL)
BOTTOM—LT NICK HUN

1LT NICK HUN, A TEAM XO AT AWARDS CEMEMONY AT DONG XOAI 1967
BOTTOM—CPT BRENNAN (CENTER) AND SENIOR MEDIC SFC ED O'NEAL ON (LEFT) BEING HONORED **(COURTESY OF AMBROSE BRENNAN)**

TOP AND BOTTOM—AWARDS CEREMONY WITH CPT BRENNAN, CPT CHU AND DISTRICT CHIEF EATING LUNCH AT DONG XOAI
(COURTESY OF AMBROSE BRENNAN)

TOP—ARVN GENERAL HONORING ONE OF OUR STRIKERS AT DX
BOTTOM—RECOGNITION FOR ONE OF OUR STRIKERS FOR HEROISM AT DX (COURTESY OF AMBROSE BRENNAN)

TERRAIN AROUND DONG XOAI (NOTE BROKEN BRANCH IN CENTER)
DID CHARLIE COME THROUGH HERE? (COURTESY OF PHIL CROWELL)

CIDGE TROOPS TAKING A BREAK WHILE ON PATROL

2LT HUN BEING PROMOTED TO 1LT BY CPT AMBROSE BRENNAN AT DONG XOAI

LIFE AT DONG XOAI

As we planned our transition to Bunard, we diligently continued our pacification efforts at Dong Xoai. DX had been kept relatively safe; therefore, we had garnered a strong base of support among the local Vietnamese people.

Our SF team members would occasionally go to the village of Dong Xoai to play volleyball with the locals. As team XO, I was also the revolutionary development officer. In this capacity, I would contact various international agencies requesting assistance, and they would donate supplies such as sheets of corrugated tin and other building materials.

Procuring the blessings of the district chief, a congenial fellow who was rumored to have ties with the other side, a version of land reform was instituted and villagers began to live relatively normal lives. Provided with the right tools and materials, they were able to build their own homes and grow vegetable gardens from seeds flown in by catholic charities, per my request.

Just before Christmas of 1966, CPT Brennan was wounded and spent the holiday at the 93rd EVAC Hospital but was back at DX in time for New Year's. CPT Brennan and I spent New Year's Eve at a village party in Dong Xoai as honored guests of the district chief.

. . .

The relationships built at DX were strong but melancholy in many respects. Having fought together with the great LLDB leadership of our counterparts, CPT Chu and LT Trieu, we knew that changes were in the offing. The trust that we had built in combat and fostered through the mundane tasks of just administering to the needs of 500 CIDG and their families would have to be repeated in our new camp.

Among these were pay issues, logistics, and medical considerations. With regard to pay, as the A Team XO, I would pick up several million "piasters" of Vietnamese currency to be utilized for CIDG pay, various camp projects, and death gratuity. The latter was paid to the families of fallen strikers. The protocol for paying the strikers was to turn the required amount over to the LLDB and for the team XO to watch as the LLDB camp commander and his XO paid the troops standing in line.

Early on in November 1966, while observing this ritual for about 15 minutes, I decided it was demeaning to CPT Chu and LT Trieu for me to be out there supervising their responsibilities. Accordingly, I went in the team house to attend to other matters. If they were inclined to manipulate the funds to their advantage, I couldn't have detected it anyway. Moreover, this gesture was to build trust between our team and the LLDB leadership.

There is a concept in Asian culture of "saving face," where one does not embarrass another needlessly. If you trust your life to your fellow warriors, would you not trust them with legal tender? While I am certain this system was abused in some camps, I don't feel it was in ours. CPT Brennan, who had served a six-month SF tour in Vietnam prior, noticed that I was not monitoring the pay line and complimented me on my decision.

. . .

Another part of everyday life at DX was the birth of babies to the CIDG wives, usually at night. SFC Ed O'Neal was our only medic for a time and would wake me to help with the deliveries if I was not out on a combat operation. Ed was an experienced SF medic, and undaunted by the task, having saved the lives of numerous combat wounded CIDG on the battlefield.

I think that Ed liked to call upon my assistance because I could readily follow directions. In addition, I think he liked the role reversal of a sergeant telling a lieutenant what to do.

One night, a young girl of perhaps 15 was brought to our dispensary in labor. The baby had crowned, so that part of the infant's head could be seen. The patient was a small, Asian girl whose labor had stopped because the baby was unable to fit through the birth canal. Being in great pain, Ed gave her a morphine injection and rather than doing a caesarian delivery, bringing more complications, he decided to make an incision to widen the birth canal sufficiently to allow the baby to exit.

My job was to put one finger of my surgically gloved hand in the rectum and one in the vagina to ensure that the scalpel did not pierce through the bowel as the incision was made. The procedure was successful and the healthy baby came out and cried, as did his striker father who had witnessed the birth of his son. Ed stitched up the mother and by morning, she was able to leave our little A Team makeshift operating room.

The young mother brought her new baby by on several occasions to see "*Bac si* Ed O'Neal." Translated into English, *Bac si* means doctor. Special Forces medics are indeed very special.

. . .

SF A Team camps, by their very nature, were isolated, dangerous places. However, when there was an opportunity for a breather from the war, my responsibility as primary logistician would find me at C Team HQ in Bien Hoa, coordinating the acquisition of food and supplies and attending to budget matters for the CIDG pay.

Often while there, I would take the short hop to Saigon with my fatigue pockets stuffed with VC flags provided by a helpful seamstress at DX. With these flags stained with chicken blood and a number of Montagnard crossbows, I was able to barter for almost anything in the overstocked Saigon depots of 1967. The navy yard was particularly productive, for as soon as a sailor saw the beret and the bow, he would retrieve several cases of steaks from the CONEX cooler and a deal was struck. Captured AK-47 and SKS rifles were reserved for chopper pilots for various other considerations.

Long Binh, a ward of the city of Bien Hoa, was the location of a large US Army logistics base and a source of supplies. Outside the gates of Long Binh, as was typical of most towns located by military bases, existed a carnal world of massage parlors, dance halls, and bars where one could enjoy their Saigon tea with the ladies when all work at the rear was done.

This was also the home of the 93rd Evac Hospital, and the nurses of Vietnam were here. These were a special breed of women having first seen the horrors of war up close. Not enough good things can be said to honor these Angels of Mercy who were able to bring much care and solace to the homesick wounded, their "round eyes" perhaps reminding the men of their wives and girlfriends back home.

I recall an evening jaunt to the 93rd by jeep from Bien Hoa. As a second lieutenant, I accompanied three captains to the officer's club, one of whom was our C Team doctor. The music was blaring and the high-pitched voices of "round eyes" filled the air as we knocked on the entrance door. Scrutinized through the peephole, our berets did not impress them in the least, and access was denied.

We noticed a MEDEVAC chopper land on the large red cross next to the club. We all approached the pilot and informed him with some urgency that we needed a stretcher and a body bag. This time, the berets worked and our request was accommodated.

Placing Doc Chase in the body bag, we returned to the club and knocking on the door again, we asked if there was a doctor in the house. Taking the stretcher and the occupied bag inside, several doctors quickly helped me open it up. Doc Chase then raised his hand, stating that he needed a drink. Our clever humor was not lost on the medicos, and access to the club was quickly granted.

There was a woman seated at the bar by her lonesome who happened to be a full colonel. My three captain companions advised me that she was in need of company. I approached the colonel, who was likely twice my age, and asked to join her. While the three captains danced and frolicked with the younger women, the colonel and I talked for several hours, after which, she asked me to escort her to her quarters. At the air-conditioned trailer, we hugged and said good night. It was a cathartic moment for both of us, and I believe a better one than that experienced by my senior cohorts.

...

I would be amiss not to tell of a few brave men with whom I served at Dong Xoai; having already mentioned SFC Ed O'Neal and SGT Phillip Crowell, not to forget our Vietnamese SF counterparts, CPT Chu and LT Trieu. Our team sergeant, MSG Robert M. Browning, was a large Texan who cared deeply about the mission and the members of his team. SSG Larry K. Jackson, our commo man, was both brave and exceptionally effective in finding and eliminating the enemy. SSG Larry B. "Stik" Rader, who later went to the mobile guerrilla force, fought the enemy with stealth in the Viet Cong controlled "Forbidden Zone."

It was also my privilege to have SGT Jimmy R. Browder accompany me on my first five-day combat operation in October 1966, soon after my arrival. The five-day mission took us south about twenty kilometers, close to the US 1st Infantry Division base at Phuoc Vinh. We encountered booby-trapped artillery rounds in the trees on Rang Rang Road and sniper fire that subsided when we went to the sound of the guns.

Jimmy and I later fought effectively together, along with SGT Philip Crowell, during one of our numerous forays into Bunard, a Viet Cong enclave where we later were to build a fighting camp. These fine, young SF NCOs would bravely go anywhere to accomplish the mission, and once the shooting started, they went in with guns blazing. Sadly, Jimmy Browder has since passed away.

Captains Charles Steinmetz and Ambrose Brennan did more than their share, leading our A Team on highly dangerous missions in enemy territory with virtually no designated outside support. These fine officers, although uniquely dissimilar in personality, were extremely competent, caring, and brave. Their "can do" spirit and desire to take the fight to the enemy resulted in a team synergism where heroism was the norm rather than the exception.

...

We didn't have much in the way of ritual in the Special Forces, but with all the talk of death and combat, there is one little custom perhaps worth mentioning. It was generally understood that a new man, fresh and unbloodied from his training in the States, had to earn his "chops." This was a way he came to be accepted and trusted by his fellow soldiers. Just as Native Americans might "count coup" or collect scalps to prove himself worthy in battle, those serving in combat had to likewise prove themselves ready and be acknowledged for it.

When a new man returned from the battlefield for the first time after registering his first kill, he was welcomed back to camp with an informal ceremony. All of his comrades received him by lining up and kissing him in the ear, affectionately referring to him thereafter as a *"sweet MF!"*

This might seem a little irreverent or unsettling to some who have never experienced the comradery that exists between combat soldiers having to rely upon each other for their very lives. This doesn't mean there was no discipline in the camps because there was, but for just this moment, a small but significant moment, there was this ritual of war—as important as any promotion or awarding of medals. War and the ways of the warrior can be extraordinary indeed.

TOP ROW—PHIL CROWELL AT DONG XOAI
BOTTOM—LT HUN XO AT DONG XOAI

1LT HUN (RIGHT) AT DONG XOAI WITH PSYCH OPS OFFICER FROM NHA TRANG AT MONTAGNARD VILLAGE—1966

TERRAIN AROUND DONG XOAI A-342 SF CAMP
(COURTESY OF PHIL CROWELL)

1LT HUN MEETING THE VILLAGE MONTAGNARD CHIEF AT DX SF CAMP—1966.

TOP—SFC O'NEAL, LT TRIEU, AND OUR RECON PLATOON EXAMINING CAPTURED VC MORTARS AND MACHINE GUNS AFTER A SUCCESSFUL OPERATION
BOTTOM—THE XO 1LT HUN CLEANING THE 30 CAL. MACHINE GUN IN THE TOWER AT A-TEAM CAMP—DONG XOAI

TOP—1LT HUN HANGING OUT WITH THE "YARDS"
BOTTOM— WILD HOG SHOT FOR SUPPER BY LT HUN DURING A ROAD CLEARING OPERATION WITH OUR ONLY M-60 MACHINE GUN

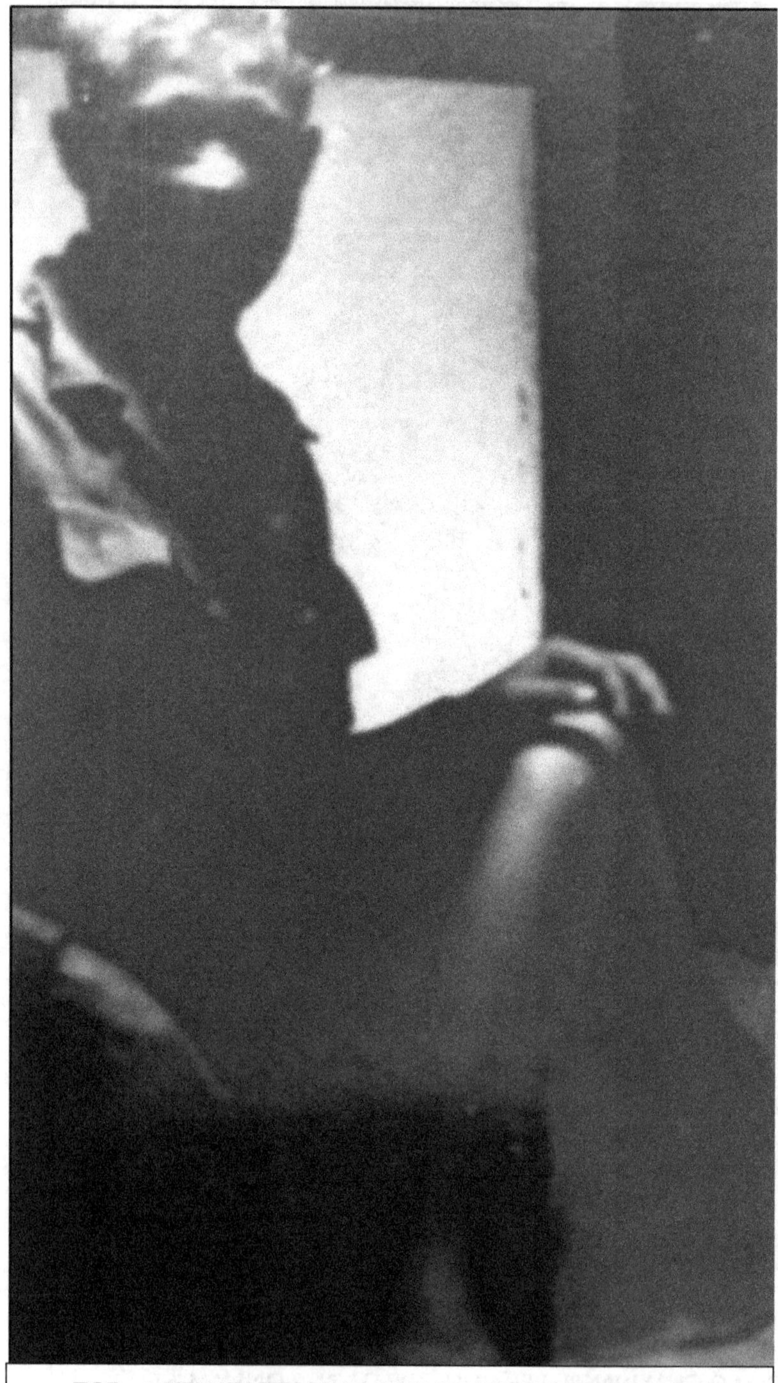

TOP—1 LT HUN HELPING OUR SENIOR MEDIC SFC ED O'NEAL DELIVER A BABY AT DONG XOAI

On occasion of Christmas Day ; we, all the Catholics of Don Luan District, will hold a party at my shop's Ngoc-Huong.

Invite Mr Capt & Mr Lt. to come to my home to share our joy, and show out our unity & our happiness to welcome Christ Day on 24th Dec '66. at 2100 H.

Your presence will be a proud to us, and be the happiness to the party too.

For The PARTY.
Headmaster of the Don Luan Elem School.

TOP—CHRISTMAS INVITATION FROM LOCAL CATHOLIC SCHOOL WE BUILT AT DONG XOAI
BOTTOM—B-52 AIR STRIKE NEAR SF CAMP DONG XOAI

CAMP BUNARD

It was late March of 1967 when our Special Forces detachment, A-342 at Dong Xoai, under the leadership of CPT Ambrose W. Brennan, was preparing to make a heliborne assault into the Viet Cong controlled village of Bunard. With an abundance of fertile rice fields and no Vietnamese government control, the region served as a resupply point for the VC/NVA heading primarily south to attack various friendly installations and troop units, including Special Forces camps. Most of the 2,500 inhabitants at Bunard lived primarily underground as it was a free-fire zone and was often attacked from the air by both US and ARVN forces.

COL Francis Kelly gave a new mission to our SF team at Dong Xoai to build a new Special Forces camp at Bunard to be dubbed A-344. The team at Dong Xoai would then take over at Bunard. Detachment A-312 from Xom Cat, an area that had largely been pacified, would now replace our team at Dong Xoai under the leadership of CPT O'Malley and LT Jim Wilde as his executive officer.

Not many Special Forces guys and teams had participated in the building of a fighting A Camp from the ground up, preceded by a mass parachute jump by a MIKE Force. I was supposed to make the jump into Bunard, called Operation Harvest Moon, because I was experienced from numerous ground operations that I had conducted. LTC Bernier, B Team commander at Song Be, wanted me along with him. Unfortunately, CPT Brennan, our A Team CO, had sent me to Saigon to purchase 200 machetes to clear vegetation at the campsite. I still have trouble forgiving him for that, even though the machetes were sorely needed.

Operation Harvest Moon, utilizing the A-503 Mobile Strike Force of irregulars, was planned and executed on April 2, 1967 by the 5th Special Forces Headquarters in Nha Trang. This so-called "country MIKE Force" consisted of 356 men, including Montagnards and US Special Forces. It was to be the first mass tactical combat jump in Vietnam since the French Foreign Legion jump at Dien Bien Phu. Under the lead of CPT Lee B. Wilson, this mass, low-level jump was conducted from a C-130 Hercules aircraft. LTC Jaquez Bernier, the B Team commander at Song Be, led a Pathfinder team to mark the drop zone after parachuting into the area himself.

The jump was immediately followed by a helicopter assault led by CPT Ambrose Brennan and our A Team members from Dong Xoai. While the initial parachute jump and helicopter landings went largely unopposed, that would change rapidly as the MIKE Force left the area, and we began construction on Camp Bunard.

Building an effective fighting camp meant having the ability to defend against daily mortar attacks, nighttime probes, and the expectation of being overrun by a large number of the enemy at any given time. Initially, about 200 CIDG, mostly Cambodians and a few Montagnards, occupied the village of Bunard. This, plus factoring in our Special Forces A Team, an SF engineer platoon from Thailand, and a Vietnamese artillery platoon with two 105mm tubes, this left us about 250 strong in an area where the NVA normally moved about in battalion strength.

We were not by any means ill-prepared, as we deployed the various weapons and defensive tactics at our disposal. This began with the emplacement of a trench network throughout the camp that would allow the men to travel to different locations with a semblance of cover and safety while under attack.

Eight CONEXs (heavy, corrugated, steel storage containers) were then brought in and firing ports cut out on three sides. These structures were placed in the trench network and sandbagged, each holding three .30 caliber machine guns with 1,000 rounds of ammunition each. Rifle cleaning rods were welded to the steel containers above the gun barrels to ensure a "grazing" field of fire. This ensured an intensive barrage of machine-gun fire concentrated just above the ground, able to cut a charging wave of enemy to bits.

Anti-personnel fléchette rounds were available for the 105mm artillery pieces, capable of sending out thousands of nail-like steel fléchettes at the enemy. Like a blast from a large shotgun, the results were devastating. It has been reported that some enemy soldiers who had been on the receiving end of these rounds were found literally nailed to the stocks of their rifles. Adding to this, we also had a 4.2-inch mortar and two 81mm mortars.

The perimeter of the camp was strung with plenty of Tanglefoot, which was a meshwork of barbed wire, and several hundred claymore mines that were essentially plastic explosives impregnated with buckshot.

Any serious attempt to overrun the camp would exact a heavy toll on the enemy. Even so, our defensive emplacements did not stop the VC from their daily mortar attacks and probes at dusk for the first two weeks. Barrels of sand were placed within easy access around the team house and trench network to keep casualties in our group to a minimum.

One evening, around dusk, while contemplating my forthcoming R&R in Bangkok, I gazed toward the north. Not to my surprise, I saw numerous flashes of light and heard the familiar "thud" of mortars leaving the tube. Realizing that it was probably a 60mm mortar, I took out my trusty compass and shot an azimuth to the flashes, even as the rounds began to land in and around our new camp. SFC Wiesnieski, who sadly passed away a number of years ago, jumped into our 4.2 mortar pit with me and began dropping several dozen HE rounds out to 1,000 meters, which was the range of the 60mm rounds the enemy were using.

A later inspection of their launch site indicated that someone had a bad day, judging by the blood trails and numerous mortar rounds left behind as they ran or crawled away. Coincidentally, our camp spent the remainder of the week in relative calm.

COL Francis Kelly, commander of the 5th Special Forces Group in Nha Trang, came to inspect our site and was pleased by what he saw. I still recall his words as he stated, "I have seen a lot of camps go in, but never one so efficiently!"

After departing, he arranged to have five pigs sent in for the CIDG to feast upon and an equal number of bottles of champagne for our A Team.

Army Intelligence had reported, and was also verified by our patrols from Bunard, that the NVA were amassing forces in the area. In mid-April, we were notified to get ready to receive reinforcements in the form of an infantry battalion from the 1st Infantry Division. As at Dong Xoai, the exceptional leadership of this great division was not going to allow us to be taken out by the VC and NVA. This region of Vietnam was a major infiltration route and resupply point for the enemy, and they thought they owned it. This was about to change, as there was a new sheriff in town in the form of our A Team and our CIDG, with the help of the very capable 1st Infantry Division.

As previously noted, the 2,500 civilian residents of the region, that had lived mostly underground, now began to visit our SF camp even as the 2nd BN of the 16th INF, 1st ID, under the command of LTC Ulatoski, began to arrive. Soon, thanks to the aggressive patrolling and killing of the now scattered enemy forces, camp construction began to flourish.

As I had done in Dong Xoai as XO and revolutionary development officer, I contacted various philanthropic organizations who provided roofing tin and other building materials for the local villagers who were ready to throw off the yoke of their oppressive communist masters.

Soon, with the assistance of the aforementioned charities, a village sprang up, replete with community and individual gardens, marking the landscape with rice, fruit, and vegetables grown from seed supplied by our team. An SF engineer detachment sent in from

Thailand, partially dammed off a nearby stream to form a thirty-acre lake that we stocked with donated fingerlings that grew quickly in the tropical climate. Before long, the locals were catching indigenous carp with short bamboo poles, using maggots as bait, providing much needed protein.

Our revolutionary development program was working, and our fighting camp was strong. The evening mortar attacks had abated as we patrolled aggressively against the Viet Cong and NVA units that now largely bypassed our camp.

CPT Ambrose Brennan had departed for the 173rd Airborne, and CPT Hugh T. Harpole, an experienced and effective officer, now led our A Team.

LT JD Rickman, who had served in the SF as an enlisted man and did a great job, became our revolutionary development officer.

MSG Browning also departed and was replaced by MSG Vernon J. Jackson, an exceptional man, whom the guys referred to as "Pappy."

SFC Sidney Jensen joined us from B-34 as our senior communications man and did a great job. I was to meet him again in the 1980s in Central America where he served in the 8th Special Forces Group.

SFC Billy Walker was our new light weapons man, and SFC Wiesnewski took care of our heavy weapons.

Our junior medic, SGT Ronald Berry, went to another team and was replaced by SP4 Paul W. Posey, who was supervised by our senior medic, SGT Thomas G. Gallant.

We now had an exceptionally stellar group of "silent professionals," as we had at Dong Xoai. We were accepted by the local community and controlled our AO, keeping the enemy on edge by killing or capturing them. We were a fortress of freedom and hope in an otherwise communist dominated landscape.

I remember having my first haircut and shave in the liberated village. We joked with the former Vietcong barber who was handling his straight razor. “There will be no tip if you cut my throat!” I exclaimed.

In late April, with a relative calm now temporarily in place, I took a quick hop to our B Team (B-34) at Song Be as I had heard that an old friend from Fort Bragg was there and about to be assigned to one of our A detachments. After landing, I ran into LTC Bernier who greeted me with his usual humorous comment, "Nice to see you, Lieutenant Hun. When are you leaving?" I responded with my usual, "Here on a mission, sir!" as we both chuckled.

Walking up to the office of CPT Gene Summers, the adjutant, there was John Rodriguez, my close friend from Bragg sitting on the steps looking forlorn. I later found out that he had been assigned to III Corps and was working his way into joining our A Team. Of course, his jungle fatigues were new and still dark green, and he was wearing the stateside "fat" of an FNG. When he saw me, it reminded him of home and he called me Nick.

Never one to be impersonal and pointing to the lone silver bar on my collar, I said, "Nick, my ass! Who can you pimp if not your friends?"

Inside, Gene Summers informed me that SSG John Rodriguez had already been assigned to another A Team. I quickly reminded him that we were on the cutting edge in a new area, badly in need of an intelligence sergeant. Still unconvinced, I further reminded him that when he was newly arrived in-country, the MIKE Force at Bu Dop, led by SF CPT Stewart and SFC Hallberg, was in the process of fighting for their lives.

At that time, LTC Bernier had considered sending Summers along as part of the relief force, but I volunteered to go instead, knowing that it was not a mission for an inexperienced officer. I recalled waiting on the airstrip with the others for the choppers to take us to Bu Dop when we received word that the mission was canceled.

CPT Summers considered the matter as a "chit" called in, and SSG Rodriguez and I left for Bunard on the next available. Sadly, CPT Stewart and SFC Hallberg are still missing in action to this day from the battle at Bu Dop. I am confident that both of these fine men died a hero's death.

When we returned to Bunard, it was back to work as LTC Ulatoski's battalion was packing up to leave. I took SSG Rodriguez out on his first five-day combat operation, along with a company of CIDG. Realizing that the 1st Infantry Division leaving the area emboldened the enemy to become more active, we made contact with a platoon of VC on the first day.

I went up to the front where the guns were blazing and told John to stay in the back with the PRC-25 radio. We killed several VC and captured one while the rest ran off. Well, here comes John in defiance of my orders! When I confronted him about it, he answered, "If you're going to be in a fight, I'm not going to stay back!" There's just no cure for some people's loyalty, I guess.

Enemy activity had continued to pick up with the departure of the 1st Infantry Division, as attested by our making regular contact with enemy forces. It had been like that at Dong Xoai.

Camp construction also continued with substantial loads of equipment and ammunition being flown in prompting our B Team to decide it was time for an inventory.

In the Special Forces, the A Team XO also serves as the S-4 or supply officer. Accordingly, I conducted an inventory, scribbling it longhand on several sheets of paper. Realizing that it was not particularly legible, and having an old Underwood typewriter in camp, I asked John to type up the inventory, knowing that at one time he had a clerk MOS.

Well, John having smelled some cordite and seen some action, he informed me that he was the team intelligence sergeant, and his responsibilities did not include typing. I tried to reason with him, explaining that on an A Team, we all had to be flexible and perform some duties not necessarily to our liking. John retorted that he did not think that was right.

Not wishing to expose the other team members to further boorish dialogue, I asked John to step outside. He seemed surprised, stating, "But you're an officer, now!" However, too proud to back down, he joined me outside where I knocked him down with a body shot and one to the jaw.

As he lay on the ground next to one of the protective barrels of sand, he asked, "Did you want that single or double-spaced?" We are good friends to this day.

. . .

Sadness and trouble are never far away in a war zone. We were not able to regain our full complement of CIDG as many stayed behind at Dong Xoai, not wishing to leave their homes and families for a jungle outpost in a foreboding place.

I also began to detect a reluctance by some of our new irregulars to conduct combat operations. Some would feign illness or look for noncombat work around the camp. I finally made the decision that all the irregulars would go on combat operations, just as the US A Team members did. This included our A Team cook, a nice, young Cambodian we named, Honcho. He had recently gotten married and they had a baby.

One day, Honcho went out on a mission with CPT Harpole and SSG John Rodriguez. Sadly, he was carried back under bamboo poles in his poncho. While we largely controlled the area, we were always subject to attacks. In this case, a Chinese claymore mine wounded several of our people and killed Honcho. I still remember his sad widow with her baby at the cremation. Heavy is the head that wears the crown.

Death in war can come in many forms and not necessarily from combat. One morning in early June, SGT Gallant asked me to go to our tiny dispensary where sick call was held. There I found a half dozen of our CIDG, bedridden and gasping for air. Overnight, a number of them had died miserable deaths.

As panic set in, our troops began flooding our clinic with symptoms, real and imagined. As we looked for a cause, we discovered that the popular fermented fish sauce, "nuoc mam," had been placed in metal cans that had previously contained brake fluid. There was death in the pot![4]

Apparently, the cans containing the highly toxic substance had not been properly cleaned prior to being filled with fish sauce. We lost a half dozen of our fighters before the issue was resolved.

The CIDG asked for lumber to build coffins for the cremations that CPT Harpole initially denied. When he went out on a combat operation the next day, I made certain that the lumber was provided, and I attended the cremations to the sound of wailing widows.

---

[4] *. . . they cried out, and said, O thou man of God, there is death in the pot. And they could not eat thereof. II Kings 4:40b (KJV)*

TOP—FOUR OF OUR SF GUYS AT BUNARD
BELOW—MASTER SERGEANT BROWNING AT BUNARD SF A TEAM

TOP—JETS TO THE RESCUE WHILE IN HEAVY CONTACT AT BUNARD—1967
BOTTOM—SSG JOHN RODRIEGUEZ, OUR "A" INTELLIGENCE NCO AT SF BUNARD

TOP—VC MORTAR ATTACK AT BUNARD SF CAMP—1967
BOTTOM—TRENCH NETWORK AT BUNARD SF CAMP

TOP—COLONEL FRANCIS J. KELLY, COMMANDER OF 5TH SPECIAL FORCES DURING INSPECTION AT BUNARD—1967
BOTTOM—BIG RED ONE (1ST INFANTRY DIVISON) AT BUNARD SF CAMP

TOP—VILLAGE BUILT BY THE 2500 VIETNAMESE WHO HAD LIVED UNDERGROUND UNTIL WE BUILT OUR CAMP AT BUNARD. I REQUESTED AND RECEIVED TIN FOR THE ROOFS. VEGETABLE GARDENS WERE GROWN FROM SEED DONATED BY CATHOLIC CHARITIES.
BOTTOM—81 MM MORTAR PIT (ONE OF TWO ALONG WITH A 4.2)

WITH THE HERD AT THE 173RD

By late May of 1967, the A detachment at the Bunard Special Forces camp had cleaned out the local VC in the area. This was accomplished with the great assistance of LTC Ulatowski's battalion of the 1st Infantry Division. The camp was now strong, and the local villagers who had lived underground were now part of the landscape in well-appointed homes by rural Vietnamese standards. Gardens marked each household, and a new lake, created courtesy of the Special Forces, was loaded with fish for them to catch. Things were going well, so it was time for new adventures.

CPT Brennan had departed for the 173rd Airborne Brigade after that unit had sustained heavy casualties in the Dak To region of the Central Highlands. I also volunteered as the call went out for experienced combat leaders to join "The Herd."

Prior to flying north for reassignment with the 173rd, I spent two weeks at Bien Hoa leading daily combat patrols of five to seven kilometers, conducting ambushes on the local VC. One day, after a successful ambush, I cleaned up and walked by a group of new soldiers under the control of the well-known and respected SFC "Blood" Burns in the local jungle school.

Noticing my Jump Wings and CIB (Combat Infantry Badge), he brought the platoon to attention, declaring the presence of an American paratrooper lieutenant, and saluted. This was high honor, indeed, because the last time I had seen him back at Fort Bragg five years prior, I was a private in Jump School and his greeting was somewhat less than cordial.

In early June of 1967, I flew by C-130 aircraft to the Special Forces camp at Dak To, assigned to the second battalion of the 503rd Airborne Infantry. There, I ran into then LTC Ludwig Faistenheimer, whom I had met while serving in the 10th Special Forces in Germany. The colonel asked me if I was doing a good job. After my positive response, he stated, "You better, or I will kick your ass!"

This was welcome banter for SF guys back in the day, particularly since we were both foreign-born Americans. He being from Germany and myself from Hungary, who later had lived as a refugee in Germany. Now in his nineties, I hope to see him again in Vegas at the next Special Operations reunion, as I have for several years. The beret is very special, as are those who wear it.

The next day, I met LTC Partain, 2nd Battalion commander, and his executive officer, MAJ Watson. In the small tent by the oft-rocketed Dak To airstrip, the colonel had the look of one who had seen his soldiers suffer and die.

In early June, a large NVA force had overrun A Company, killing more than ninety soldiers and most of its officers. Many were murdered by the enemy as they lay wounded. An attitude of no quarter, asked or given, developed among the paratroopers of our unit.

During my intake interview, MAJ Watson looked at me and exclaimed, "It looks like we have a hard charger here!" Before I was to meet LTC Partain, MAJ Watson enjoined me not to ask the colonel for anything. My cheeky response was, "I was just going to ask for a three-day pass." His puzzled expression revealed the soul of a man who had lost all of his humor to the crucible of war.

I was to meet these fine officers again as generals, under much happier circumstances, when I was a lieutenant colonel in command of the second of my three battalions at Fort Riley, Kansas. LTC Partain was a true combat leader who cared deeply for the men he bravely led with toughness, dignity, and grace.

After MAJ Watson's initial intake interview, I drew my M16 rifle, ammunition, a rucksack, and other tools of war, including a compass, bayonet, hand grenades, both M26 fragmentation and smoke grenades of various colors. Fully loaded and wearing my rucksack, I reported to the Dak To airstrip where a Huey helicopter from "The Cowboys" (335th Assault Helicopter Company) was waiting to take me to my new home, deep in the bush. The officers of B Company, Second Battalion of the 173rd Airborne Brigade, were there waiting for the new lieutenant.

The chopper ride was exhilarating! The Cowboys, well-known for their bravado, made sure that the new LT would remember the high-speed, low-level excursion through the mountains and valleys of the Central Highlands of Vietnam. I would mimic their antics on my next tour in Nam when I would be piloting both "Slicks and guns" from June of 1969 to June of '70. Let me leave that for later.

Arriving at the B Company logger site around noon, I walked by three occupied body bags. These soldiers had been killed by friendly fire. I would find out later that this was not a rare occurrence in the Highlands. These three soldiers, killed the night before, were Walt Brinker's troops, whose personal account of Dak To appears in the next chapter.

There was much enemy contact, and the supporting artillery was firing "high angle" over the hills and valleys with limited accuracy. The monsoon rains and high humidity, that sometimes negatively affected the propellant charges, further exacerbated the issue. I have often wondered how many of our fifty-eight thousand-plus American dead died from something other than enemy action in the jungles and reeds.

The gunner and crew chief dutifully placed the three fallen soldiers in the Cowboy's chopper. As I walked away, amid the rubble of fallen trees, I was somewhat affected by the solemnity of the moment.

I asked a group of the shirtless soldiers, smoking by their foxholes, where I could find the company commander. I could not help but notice that they were clothed in filthy jungle fatigue pants and had scabs from jungle rot covering much of their faces.

One man pointed to a small campfire where I noted four individuals, equally unkempt, with three-day beards. Alas, they were the company officers. I never felt so clean! It was here that I met the company commander of the Herd for the first time, CPT Larry Willoughby, and my fellow platoon leaders, Lieutenants Cornelius, Al McDevitt, Paul Gillenwater, and Robert Philbin.

As I approached the group, proudly wearing my first lieutenant bars on my clean jungle fatigues, the captain growled, "Take your frickin' rank off!" This was, therefore, my initial introduction into my new unit. The other lieutenants later told me that they were impressed and heartened to know that there was still life outside of Dak To, where an officer can still look like an officer, and soldiers are not covered with filth.

CPT Willoughby assigned me to the weapon's platoon where my platoon sergeant was a brand new "shake and bake," E-5, buck sergeant named Jordan. Along with my newbie sergeant, I inherited eighteen soldiers who had not yet experienced enemy contact.

Whereas, in some units, the weapon's platoon would remain behind to provide fire support; but in the Herd, we humped it right alongside the rest of the company. The only difference was that we carried several M2 60mm mortars, as well as an M18 57mm recoilless rifle, and an extra M60 machine gun. Add to these the weight of three-hundred rounds of M16 ammunition and a couple of M26 fragmentation and smoke grenades; you are well loaded down. To help distribute the weight among the men, each of us also carried a couple of rounds for the M60 mortar. It was later determined, however, that this system frequently caused casualties among our own troops in the triple-canopy jungle of the Central Vietnamese Highlands.

A captain, who shall remain unnamed as he has passed on, told me to put out some rounds to cover the nightly ambush we sent out from the company perimeter. There was no enemy contact at the time, so I was very deliberate as I set up the mortar. My plan and intention was to fire well away from the guys out front on the ambush. I had seen a lot of fratricide among US units when I was in the SF and did not wish to be a contributor.

The unnamed captain, perhaps thinking, *What do lieutenants know?* decided to speed things up by firing several rounds out of one of the M60 mortars. I could immediately tell by the weak report of the rounds leaving the tube, and seeing the charges burning rather than blowing the rounds out with force, that this was not going to end well!

A squad from LT Paul Gillenwater's platoon happened to be on the receiving end of this and, consequently, three of his soldiers suffered deep gashes on their legs from shrapnel. The wounded men were brought back to the company perimeter where the medics administered first aid and morphine.

Although the wounds were not life-threatening, the painful moans and groans of the men could be heard throughout most of the night. Their suffering must be endured, however, until the Cowboys could fly them out the next day.

The next five months brought some of the heaviest fighting of the war to the Highlands, and I would participate in four of them before ending my first tour in the Nam. Sadly, much of my platoon of new guys stayed and fought on Hill 875 in November of '67 when the Herd took heavy casualties. Although I have attended numerous Herd reunions, I have never run into any of the eighteen men in my platoon. It does give me some comfort knowing that they were alive when I departed in October of '67.

We typically operated in company strength of about one-hundred-twenty troopers with four or five officers, depending on whether Father Watters, our battalion's Catholic chaplain, or LT Tom Dorsey, our artillery forward observer came along with us. These good men often humped the hills with us, and I had a lot of fun chiding Tom about being stuck with a bunch of dirty grunts not befitting a refined artillery officer. He took it in stride.

Chaplain Watters was a special man. I can still see him tending to and praying over our wounded during several enemy contacts as bullets were flying and rocket-propelled grenades were exploding. He was very brave and committed to taking care of our troopers' spiritual as well as physical needs. He normally carried extra C rations and gave them to our soldiers when we could not be resupplied due to enemy contact or foul weather.

Chaplain Watters died a hero's death in November of 1967 on Hill 875, taking care of the wounded when a stray bomb landed on them. He was most deservedly awarded the Congressional Medal of Honor. While assigned to The United States Military Academy at West Point, I was blessed to lead a color guard honoring his service at his hometown in New Jersey in 1978.

It was a different war in the Highlands. The NVA were thick as fleas in the area, well trained, and equipped. Whereas we usually operated at company strength, the enemy amassed large forces to engage and isolate us. We passed numerous fortified areas on a daily basis, replete with bunkers, sometimes occupied and other times not.

We had numerous significant contacts with the enemy, essentially, because we were on their patch, and they were not happy about it. I vividly recall one such engagement in late July of 1967. It was around noon on the 21st and, as usual, we had passed several unoccupied NVA battalion-sized bunker complexes. LT Gillenwater's second platoon was in the lead with our German shepherd scout dog named Heidi, and her handler.

We climbed up a mountain that had stairs and a handrail emplaced by the NVA. My weapon's platoon followed LT Gillenwater's second platoon, and the command group was wedged between us when Heidi alerted. LT Gillenwater reported the alert to CPT Willoughby who ordered a "recon by fire." LT Gillenwater quickly put a squad on line and opened up on the, yet unseen, enemy.

The crescendo of automatic weapons fire was much too heavy for the squad online, and the captain yelled that it was enough. Paul Gillenwater calmly retorted back, "It's not just us!" as green tracers flew over our company, along with the "swoosh" of rocket-propelled grenades clearly audible. Apparently, our weapons fire had triggered an ambush set for us by the NVA.

I called CPT Willoughby on the PRC-25 radio and asked, "Where do you want me?" His immediate response was, "Get your ass up here!" I gave him a "Roger!" and handed the handset back to my RTO, Private Pender, a black soldier from Philadelphia. Much to our surprise, the handset exploded in his hand! I can remember seeing that his lips were moving but no sound was coming out of his mouth; a normal reaction for one's initial contact with the enemy.

As neither one of us was bleeding, the sniper had obviously missed. I ordered PVT Pender to attach another handset. As he dutifully complied, I noticed that my untested soldiers were laying on the ground looking terrified.

Instinctively, looking over my right shoulder above us toward some high bamboo among the trees, I saw something tan or brown move slightly. I grabbed the M60 machine gun from the gunner and began firing. After several short bursts, the NVA sniper was upside down in the bamboo where he had fallen, quite dead. This served to hearten our platoon for the coming fight.

Handing the M60 back to the gunner, I gave the order to attack! As I ran up the hill to the sound of the incoming fire, I glanced back. Alas, it was only PVT Pender, myself, and a young soldier from Chicago with a Polish surname that followed.

Rallying the troops, we dropped our rucksacks and charged up the hill. As we passed by, I saw Father Watters tending to several of the wounded, as well as CPT Willoughby, who was being treated for an RPG wound on his hand.

As heavy automatic weapons fire rained down on us, I again asked the captain where he wanted me. His animated response was— *"Take the frickin' hill!"* I instantly responded by putting my platoon on line, as did lieutenants' Philbin and McDevitt. Several of our seasoned NCOs shouted the order, "Grenades!" while holding their M26 "frags" high in the air. We threw our grenades!

At the sound of the detonations, we charged up the hill, firing our weapons, and screaming obscenities at the NVA who seemed surprised by our bold attack. At this point, I noticed to my right that PFC Mike Nale was bleeding from a head wound while heroically engaging the enemy with his M79 grenade launcher. The intensity of our attack at close range shocked the NVA!

Some ran, others tried to cover themselves with leaves. Most of them died over their weapons. CPT Willoughby called for prisoners to be taken, but that did not happen. After the events of June when much of the A Company of our battalion was lost, some killed as they lay wounded, prisoners were hard to come by. To my knowledge, no NVA were murdered on that day as they had done to A Company. However, this reinforced NVA platoon would never fight again.

Among our wounded was Heidi, our German shepherd, with some light RPG shrapnel wounds in her behind. Her alert and LT Gillenwater's sage response saved many lives that day. Heidi left by chopper with her handler for treatment, along with a dozen of our troopers. On the lighter side, as this battle ended, we policed the battlefield discovering numerous M26 grenades that our young soldiers had thrown. In their excitement, however, they had failed to first remove the pins before throwing.

Awards for valor were later issued, including to PFC Mike Nale and LT Paul Gillenwater, among others. I can still see Paul bravely leading his soldiers as they all engaged the enemy at close range. Mike Nale and I became close after the war while attending several Herd reunions, along with "Doc" Cotney, one of our heroic medics.

Sadly, Mike, a singularly brave soldier, left us several years ago when he lost his final battle to cancer. I communicate often with his son, Kane Nale, a great man in his own right. Apples don't fall far from the trees, as the saying goes.

Paul Gillenwater continued leading soldiers in an exemplary manner, primarily at the platoon level, for the rest of his first tour and came to visit me at Fort Lewis, Washington. Like many of us,

Paul returned to Vietnam and had a stellar career as a US Army officer. Upon retirement, he ran the jail system in Nevada. We are close friends to this day, and I plan to see him this fall at the Special Operations reunion in Las Vegas where he and his wife reside.

The remainder of the tour was pretty much the same as all that had gone on before. Enemy contact occurred with regularity, as well as unfortunate fatal incidents.

One particular day, one of our units was setting up a hasty landing zone for resupply. They had cut down a large tree that accidently landed on a soldier who was out providing security. As his crushed body was being removed, we could see that his head was twice the normal size, and his short-cropped, blond hair was dark red.

Normally, officers did not accompany their soldiers on nightly squad-sized ambushes outside the company perimeter. As we only had eighteen soldiers in my platoon, I went with them on night ambushes, leaving back a small element to tend the 60mm mortars for fire support.

We went out the usual thousand meters and set up our ambush on a well-worn trail, obviously used by the NVA. As I had mostly new men, I set up the claymore mines myself and told PVT Pender to look after the M60 machine gun. As I bent over to emplace a claymore, there was a short burst of machine-gun fire, and I saw one of the orange tracer rounds fly by much too close to me. Looking back, I saw my faithful RTO, Private Pender, with a terrified look on his face. Complying with my misguided order to get on the machine gun, he tried to chamber a round in the M60 that fires from the open bolt position.

Earlier, he had been slow responding to an order from SGT Jordan and was ordered to dig a 6x6 hole in the ground; standard punishment for minor infractions in the bush. I had considered that perhaps he was angry about this and tried to kill me. However, that clearly was not the case because he absolutely needed me more than I needed him. Besides, he was a great soldier, albeit still largely inexperienced.

We spent the night listening to the "F—k You" lizards with no enemy contact. Private Pender, however, heard all manner of things. When my turn came to sleep, and knowing that we had trip flares out, I told him to wake me if the enemy came along. After the second time he woke me, asking to engage an enemy that was not there, I told him to take out his bayonet and kill them with that when they get close. I slept well and had a good chuckle at wake up seeing my RTO, wideawake, holding his bayonet. War has its humor!

On the same track, but less humorous, we had worked our way back to a firebase and were looking forward to coming in and perhaps getting a hot meal, and maybe even a beer. Along with A Company, we looked down with longing at the GP medium tents and 105mm artillery tubes, as well as the field kitchen in a valley about a click from us. To our chagrin, however, the order came for us to stay out and provide security, which angered our soldiers and, to be frank, the officers and NCOs as well.

At the crack of dawn, however, a hellacious rocket and mortar attack hit the firebase which caused our soldiers to cheer derisively. While no one was killed, there were numerous wounded paratroopers, including MAJ Watson, our battalion executive officer. He ostensibly made the decision to keep us out, thereby saving many lives. Thank you, sir, and RIP!

CPT Jack Price took command of B Company in August of 1967. A no-nonsense leader, he had served in the Herd on a prior tour and was wounded. As an interesting sidenote, he had actually appeared in Playboy Magazine with Playboy Bunny, Joan Collins, who visited him in the hospital.

As we aggressively pursued the NVA, CPT Price was determined to protect his soldiers from disease as well as the enemy. Newly instituted policies at the firebases included, haircuts down to the skin, along with facial and other camouflage in the bush.

There were fines instituted for inadvertent weapons discharges and other misdeeds. Moreover, smoking on the move was prohibited which added to the stress. Even before CPT Price had arrived, the punishment for leaving your weapon behind was serving all night alone as an outpost, armed only with a bayonet.

Some of the recently assigned soldiers, affectionately referred to as FNGs, had heard the stories of the loss of A Company. This only exacerbated the feelings of impending doom as we walked through NVA base camps with the smell of death hanging heavy in the air.

At an overnight logger site, two soldiers shot themselves in the foot to get out of the bush where they thought they would surely die. Stress took its toll in other ways. One soldier, caught smoking, turned his M-16 rifle toward CPT Price and went into a verbal tirade about the new policies. The CPT responded by chambering a round in the shotgun he carried, saying, "Don't miss!" as several of the NCOs and I stepped between them. The soldier was reassigned to another unit back at Dak To.

I recall an incident where one of LT Bob Philbin's NCOs did not come forward to lead his soldiers during a firefight. Bob threw him out of his platoon, stating he could go and sleep outside the perimeter. Seeing the forlorn look on his face, I invited him to my platoon. He became one of my better NCOs and was quite aggressive during the next firefight. If there are things worse than fear, being an outcast might be one of them, particularly when all you have is each other.

There were lighter moments. Heidi and her handler typically stayed with us in the weapons platoon area as our company dug in each night. While preparing my fighting position for the night, I touched a web gear hanging from a tree that was in my way. I heard a low-level growl and felt slobber on my wrist. Heidi was guarding her handler's equipment and gently reminded me of that fact. The look in her eyes seemed to say, "I am sorry but, please!" Heidi and I had a special relationship as we bonded often over C ration crackers. I know she loved me as I did her.

CPT Price did an excellent job under very trying conditions, and as the troops became adjusted to the new commander, things went much better. I vividly recall coming in to Dak To for a break on August 18th. As we began to lay out our equipment to dry and dig in for the night, here come the Cowboys over the runway with troops in tiger suits hanging from ropes. Even as they bounced a couple of the guys on the concrete runway, we knew this was not a good omen. As the radio began to crackle, we got the word!

A long-range reconnaissance team from the 17th Calvary Regiment had been discovered by the enemy and attacked. While the team got away, the team leader did not. Our company was told to go and get him out NOW! As this was an emergency short-term mission, only guns and ammo needed to be carried.

With dutiful compliance, we made our way across the runway where the Cowboys were waiting to take us to the scene of the extraction. We went in hot with the door gunners firing away as we landed at the base of the hill where the team had been attacked. Upon landing, we could see a squad-sized unit of Viet Cong in their typical black pajamas walking through a valley several kilometers away.

After calling in artillery on the departing VC, we climbed the hill where the contact occurred. As darkness set in and a heavy rain began to fall, we made camp for the night. However, since we had no shelter halves and very few ponchos, we spent a miserable night in the rain.

Leaning against a tree, soaked to the bone and freezing, I checked my watch many times that night until the crack of dawn brought some much-needed relief. If anyone ever tells you that it does not get cold in the tropics, don't believe them.

We did find the body of SSG Charles James Holland who had bravely covered his team as they departed under fire. He went back up the hill to retrieve a radio they had dropped, where he died a hero's death engaging the enemy. Later, SSG Holland was posthumously promoted to SFC and awarded the Distinguished Service Cross, our nation's second highest award for valor.

. . .

LT Phil Bodine, another singularly outstanding officer, replaced Paul Gillenwater as the second platoon leader in early August. Phil had been a platoon leader, and part of the relief force in C Company, under the command of CPT Ron Leonard in June when A Company was isolated and mostly destroyed by a large NVA force. In spite of their best efforts, they could not get to A Company in time to save them and had to deal with the sad carnage left in the wake of the attack.

Later, Phil Bodine bravely led his platoon until severely wounded on November 13th. He had 41 puncture wounds on his body when he was finally evacuated the next day, earning him his first Silver Star and several Bronze Stars for valor.

Phil and I were at the Infantry Advanced Course together at Fort Benning, GA. From there, the army sent us to college to get our degrees, then to helicopter flight school in 1969. From there, it was back to Disneyland Far East in Vietnam with the 145th Combat Aviation Battalion, where Phil flew Cobra gunships in the 334th Attack Helicopter Company, and I flew B Model Huey gunships in the 190th Assault Helicopter Company. Neither of us finished our flight plans each time we took off. We can leave that for later.

Friendships that are forged in war last a lifetime. Particularly when mortal combat, at close range with the smell of cordite heavy in the air, is the order of the day. Nowhere is the measure of a man taken as quickly as on the battlefield. Now, some fifty years later, there are eleven of us old guys left from the second battalion, 173rd Airborne Brigade in Vietnam. We are close friends that bond annually, telling slightly embellished stories of glory and gore as we imbibe the nectar of the gods.

...

LT Bob Philbin, from New York, had served as an instructor at the Ranger School prior to joining the Herd. We had a shared linage as his grandmother was Hungarian. We enjoyed a good laugh over an occasional beer with Kolbász, a Hungarian sausage that my sister would send to me. It bothered us little that it was covered in mold because we considered it penicillin.

Sometime in August, we went to Dak To, laid out our gear to dry, and walked over to get cleaned up at the field shower that had been set up. As we came out of the shower, carrying our M16 rifles with magazines loaded, we were approached by an unnamed sergeant-major all starched up in his jungle fatigues. We were not wearing any rank, so he wasn't aware that we were officers.

The sergeant-major barked at us, in a loud voice, that we are not to have our magazines in our weapons! I smiled as I sensed that this would not go well for the sergeant-major. Sure enough, LT Philbin went "New York" on him, the tirade beginning with, "You douche bag!" and ending with words to the effect that, "Where you hang out, magazines may not be needed, but in our world, they are essential!" I noticed the senior NCO's heels come together as he saluted, departing post haste. Not all lieutenants are alike.

TOP—PFC CHARLES A. MARSHALL RECEIVING AN AWARD AT DAK TO
BOTTOM—LT TOM REMINGTON AT DAK TO—1967
(PHOTOS COURTESY OF 1LT ALLEN MCDEVITT)

1. 1LT McDevitt in UH-1 outboard side
en-route to asault Hill 810 - 10 Nov 1967
2. Map reconnaisance Tuy Hoa 5 Nov 1967

3. 3rd Platoon B Co 2/503rd re-supply
distribution Tuy Hoa RVN 4 Nov 1967
Prior to return to Dak To 5 Nov 1967
4. SFC Jackson - 3rd Platoon Sgt

5. SFC Jackson, SSG Fitzgerald
Platoon Sergeants B Co. 2/503rd
Staging for transport to Dak To
5 Nov 1967 - Photos:
SP4 Wako Cotney 3rd Platoon Medic

MGR CHARLES J. WATTERS
JAN 17, 1927—NOV 19, 1967
CHAPLAIN/ 173RD SPT BN
MORTALLY WOUNDED AT
DAK TO, VIETNAM
AWARDED THE
CONGRESSIONAL
MEDAL OF HONOR

173RD ABN OFFICERS REUNION
L-R: NICK HUN, PAUL GILENWATER, MATT HARRISON, BARTH O'LEARY

WALT BRINKER'S WAR

One of my very good friends, who also served with the Herd at Dak To, was First Lieutenant Walt Brinker. We still keep in touch. He, and author William Brown, have generously given me permission to use material written for WALT BRINKER'S WAR, from VOL 3 of WILLIAM F. BROWN'S series, OUR VIETNAM WARS. The following are from Walt's own words:

In 1962, I was admitted to West Point, graduated in the Class of 1966, and was commissioned an infantry officer. After Airborne training and Ranger School, most of my class were assigned to troop duty where we learned how to work with NCOs and soldiers before being sent to Vietnam.

More than 100 in my West Point class were in Vietnam as platoon leaders within one year after graduation. I arrived in June 1967, assigned as a rifle platoon leader in A Company, 2d Battalion, 503d Infantry, 173d Airborne Brigade, the "Sky Soldiers." They were the first US combat brigade to arrive in-country. The brigade's combat battalions were up at Dak To in the Central Highlands, where the mountainous terrain was covered with triple-canopy jungle infested with leeches, thick bamboo, very aggressive mosquitoes, and the North Vietnamese Army, the NVA. I had been in Vietnam a week, waiting to go through the unit's 5-day in-country orientation, when the company I was assigned to suffered heavy casualties in a battle with a larger NVA unit – 76 killed, including all the platoon leaders, two of whom were West Point classmates I had seen the week before. This confirmed that we were playing hardball, and I had better focus on being the best platoon leader possible.

Arriving at Dak To, I saw the burned, scarred side of the mountainside where air strikes had tried in vain to help my company, survivors of which had since been withdrawn and were assigned as perimeter defense for the fire support base. It was monsoon season, and by the time I reported to my company commander that night in his small hex tent to be briefed on his SOPs, I was soaking wet and muddy from setting up my hooch in the driving rain. As I left that meeting and went back out into the darkness and driving rain, I recall telling myself, "This is going to be a long (bleeping) year."

A week or so later, my newly reconstituted company was sent out on a "shakedown operation." Jittery from the earlier catastrophe, the CO ordered us to form a perimeter on a ridgeline when the lead platoon encountered the enemy. C Company was also in contact a kilometer or so away, and 105-millimeter artillery was firing in support. One of its six artillery pieces fired two rounds by mistake right into my company's position. The first round came screeching toward my platoon and landed ten feet away, killing three of my men. Their squad leader and I heard it coming and we flopped safely to the ground just before it impacted. Seconds later the second round landed in the middle of the company perimeter killing and wounding several more and severely wounding the company commander. In spite of this incident, I later became a big fan of close-in artillery support and used it often.

My first big fire fight occurred near Tuy Hoa, after being reassigned to B Company as part of a major reorganization, while on a platoon patrol in heavily vegetated high ground overlooking another fire support base. During that fight, which seemed to last forever, one of my squad leaders, right next to me, was shot between the eyes and killed. I killed the shooter with a couple of hand grenades. After the fight, my troops told me they approved of the way I had led the platoon; this was huge positive reinforcement.

My last big battle on that tour was on November 12, 1967, one of the early fights during the major, infamous "Battle of Dak To." My platoon position was coming under attack, but I couldn't determine whether my soldiers on a forward observation post (OP) had come back into our position. Since I didn't want my men to fire until I knew the OP was in, I scampered toward them to bring them back. My radio operator (RTO), Art Fleming, then shouted that the OP was in, but their radio had been shot out. He also told me that there were five NVA soldiers in a bomb crater just outside the perimeter ahead of me.

About that time, I saw those NVA raise their AK-47s above the edge of the crater and spray fire toward my platoon. My preferred solution was to have the squad leader closest to the crater handle the problem; however, the extreme and unprecedented din from all the gunfire and explosions didn't allow any voice communication. So, I figured it was going to be my "show-time" – the reason the Army paid me "the big bucks."

The bomb crater the NVA were hiding in was surrounded by scraggly bamboo and about twenty feet from me. I would have preferred to lob grenades over the bamboo at them. However, grazing incoming machine gun fire about a foot above the ground would have hit me, and throwing the grenades in low risked bouncing them off the bamboo. So, Plan B! I told two men to my left to cover me while I crawled closer to the crater and intended to flip grenades into the crater through the small gaps in the bamboo. I was about halfway there, when a mortar round, certainly NVA, landed two feet to my left, splattered my left side with shrapnel, and wounded the men who were there covering me.

My RTO, responding to a call from my company commander, told him I was seriously injured and needed a medic. Somehow my platoon suppressed the enemy fire and drove them off. Since my legs were OK, I was able, with help from the medic, to stumble back to cover behind a thick felled teak tree.

A major artery on the left side of my neck had been severed. The medic saved me by clamping it. I later learned I had lost two quarts of blood and the plasma injected via IV tube prevented my going into shock. I also had a "sucking chest wound," treated by placing a piece of plastic sheet over the wound to seal off air loss, and by laying me on my left side to enable my right lung to function without also filling with blood. Heavy enemy fire prevented bringing in a medevac helicopter for an hour, until Air Force fighter-bombers arrived and plastered the enemy positions.

Meanwhile, I stayed down behind the tree, as enemy bullets ground into it, and spoke with the company commander by radio. My main concern was that we would be overrun, and I would not be able to defend myself. Luckily that didn't happen. When the first evacuation helicopter arrived, several litter cases were loaded aboard behind the pilot and I was jammed into a tight space sitting next to the door gunner. As we lifted off, he was firing his M-60 machine gun, and green enemy tracer rounds zipped past us. It was quite a ride! A sad note: the medic who saved me was killed the next day.

At 71st Evac Hospital, the surgeon, Doctor Kurris, removed my spleen and 1/3 of my pancreas, tied off my severed left neck artery, and left me with an impressive array of surgical scars on my neck, lower and left chest, shoulder, forearm, and buttock. The back of my left hand is still partially numb.

They made me stay in Vietnam until my fever went down. That was followed by two more weeks at the 249th General Hospital at Camp Drake in Japan before I was flown to Walter Reed Hospital in DC and allowed to go home on convalescent leave. Christmas 1967, with my family, was my best ever. I had survived and apparently would recover okay. But as I walked around shopping centers before Christmas, my mind remained on that battlefield. I couldn't comprehend the stark contrast between the mall and the jungle, and I remember thinking what boring lives all these folks led.

LTC WALT BRINKER RETURNED TO VIETNAM IN 1969 AS A CAPTAIN AND WAS EXCEPTIONALLY SUCCESSFUL COMMANDING A RIFLE COMPANY IN THE 25th INFANTRY DIVISION. WALT RETIRED FROM THE ARMY AS A LIEUTENANT COLONEL IN 1990.

THE 190TH AHC

I would like to dedicate this chapter to Danney Pickard, who was a crew chief at the 190th AHC, and his twin brother, Richard James Pickard "Dickey," who died in Vietnam with the 180th AHC.

After completing helicopter flight training in June of 1969, it was back to Vietnam with the 145th Combat Aviation Battalion in Bien Hoa. Initially assigned to the 68th Assault Helicopter Company, I was to fly with them primarily as a copilot.

In early September, while we were flying the command-and-control ship, inserting South Vietnamese soldiers near Xuan Loc, a tragic event transpired which cost the life of our crew chief. I leave out names and details, but on September 7th, I requested a transfer out of the unit and ended up as the battalion motor officer. Just what every chopper pilot wants to do in a combat zone, right?

I did get to fly a few missions, including some with my first battalion commander, COL John J. Top, who was an outstanding officer. I would meet him again decades later in Pennsylvania at a battalion reunion organized by one of our great crew chiefs, Danney Pickard, of the 190th AHC. To this day, he and his wife, who he affectionately calls "Mama," have worked tirelessly for many years to keep us all connected.

Having successfully completed my purgatory in the motor pool in November of 1969, I received an early Christmas present. COL Seleskar, a great leader on his second tour and our new battalion commander, appointed me platoon commander of the Gladiators in the 190th AHC.

A typical day in the 190th would begin with going to the flight line to perform a preflight inspection of two or three of the B Model Huey gunships that would be flown on that day. The crew chief and gunner would already be there, checking the choppers and ensuring that the weapons and other systems were functional.

As a rule, the Gladiator platoon would fly troop escort missions with the Slicks that carried US, South Vietnamese, and other allied soldiers on combat assaults. As the troop carriers approached, artillery would "prep the LZ," after which, we would make a gun run with miniguns. One of our gunships would then go to ground level to visually inspect the landing zone for enemy bunkers in the tree line.

On one such occasion, my chopper was about three feet off the ground in a LZ that had been prepared by artillery. I had spoken with the artillery officer in charge, who informed me that they had finished shooting. Additionally, I observed a white phosphorous round land, signaling the end of the fire mission. We were then surprised when a 105mm round landed about thirty yards behind us. I called Redleg with a "WTF?" and his response was, "Oops!" As stated, there were many ways to die if someone was not watching over you. On the days when no troop insertions were planned, the guns were on the flight line, ready for action, if needed by ground troops, Special Forces, or any allied soldiers or facilities.

Our B Model Hueys (UH-1B) were outfitted with "hog pods" capable of holding thirty-eight 2.75 rockets, or a combination of eighteen rockets and two miniguns that could fire one thousand 7.62mm rounds per minute. In the back of the chopper, the crew chief and the gunner manned their own M60 machine guns. They were not only our eyes beneath us but also covered us coming out of gun runs.

As we normally started our attacks on the enemy ground troops from five-hundred feet, it was hard to miss. Flying through the dense smoke of exploding rockets brought special thrills as we broke out of our runs around treetop level. Typically, the men in the back, the crew chief and gunner, were hanging on their "monkey straps," firing their "free guns" to cover our collective behinds, with an occasional grenade thrown in for good measure.

These men were a special breed. Many had prior combat tours on the ground or in the air and had "extended" for this dangerous but exhilarating duty. We were a welcome sight to both the US and South Vietnamese ground troops. As for the untold numbers of unlucky enemy, the "skull in helmet with cross rockets" of the Gladiator symbol would be their final vision.

. . .

My time in Vietnam during 1969 and '70 as a pilot brought many new adventures for a guy who thought he had seen it all; fighting on the ground as a Special Forces lieutenant on two A Teams in the III Corps at Dong Xoai and Bunard, and as an infantry platoon leader at Dak To with the Herd. Revisiting III Corps from the air in places where I fought on the ground was particularly rewarding.

By early 1970, the VC and NVA had infiltrated much of the area and probed and attacked the Special Forces camps with regularity. MAJ Ben Aiken, whom I had met in Bad Tolz, Germany with the 10th Special Forces, was the B Team commander at Song Be, about thirty kilometers north of Dong Xoai. A dashing cavalry officer, he was just what was needed at Song Be.

On one occasion, the target rich environment around Song Be produced a column of the enemy on the march. As we attacked with our heavy fire team of B Model gunships in this "free-fire zone," our rockets flew and miniguns roared, causing pith helmets to sail in all directions.

Ben and I were to meet again later in the States at the Infantry Officers Advanced Course at Fort Benning, GA. He expressed his gratitude for the support from above while we reminisced over beer at the officer's club. Ben later left to attend the Armor Advanced Course, leaving me to my own devices.

Another mission took us up to the A Team at Bu Dop in the Northwest III Corps area, where Lieutenant Trieu, the heroic Vietnamese A Team executive officer from Dong Xoai, was now camp commander. Knowing where we were going, I brought along several bottles of Seagram's, but when we showed up, the camp was under mortar attack.

Later, after shooting up several enemy units, we landed. CPT Trieu, accustomed to working with me in the Special Forces, came out to greet us. His first words to me with a wide grin were, "Hun, you Air Force now?"

We reminisced about our days at Dong Xoai as A Team XOs. Sadly, it would be the last time I would see him. Such is war unfinished.

On a brighter side, I would meet LTC Dietz, the US Green Beret executive officer from that team, decades later. He served in the 19th Special Forces Group in West Virginia, and I was the senior army advisor to that venerable group of patriots.

The new year brought another surprise that would give our chopper crew something to remember. While supporting US ground troops, in contact with our rockets and miniguns in January 67, we had our hydraulic system shot out by enemy ground fire. As I was relatively new to the Gladiators, CW2 Huggins was the aircraft commander and flying when we lost control of the chopper and crashed. We got off our Mayday call and went in to a relatively open but hilly area. As we hit the ground hard, we rolled over. The rotor blades struck the ground and violently threw the aircraft, coming to rest on its left side where I sat among unexploded rockets that had broken free from the crash. The crew chief had jumped out prior to impact and was safe. Our wing man covered us as a 190th Slick came in, got us out, and flew us back to Bien Hoa.

The next morning, I woke up staring at the cockroaches on the ceiling, unable to move my legs. I took several deep breaths and grabbed my legs, one at a time, and placed them on the floor until some feeling returned. I shuffled to the dispensary, where Doc Chase examined me and said I had a compression fracture in my lumbar between L2 and L3.

Apparently, the fluid buildup from the crash injury had pressed on my spinal nerves and caused the temporary paralysis. My back and I communicate regularly, along with the doctors who did numerous spinal blocks. Fortunately, our son, Nicholas, is a chiropractor, so we go to Greenville, South Carolina to see our grandkids and get some relief.

Per protocol, I took a post-crash check ride about a week later with CW2 O'Connor, which I passed. So, it was back to the air as an aircraft commander leading light and heavy fire teams on combat assault missions, escorting the troop-laden Huey Slicks, and prepping the landing zones with our rockets and miniguns.

On one of our missions, we flew south toward IV Corps in support of the 9th Infantry, who were in contact as we arrived. A rifle platoon had engaged NVA in bunkers and had been pinned down. After they popped smoke to identify their position, we rolled in hot with rockets and miniguns. After numerous bunkers were destroyed, an NVA soldier came out of one of them, holding his AK-47 over his head. The lead aircraft was not certain if it was a gesture of surrender or a suicidal attempt to engage us. After several attempts to get him to drop his weapon by hand motions were unsuccessful, the gunner killed him with a burst from his M60 machine gun. Sadly, such is war!

On a happier note, then CPT Phil Bodine, one of the heroes I had served with in the Central Highlands in '67, was the leader of the Raiders platoon of Cobra helicopters in our battalion. Phil had left Dak To feet first after being severely wounded on Hill 875 while bravely leading his platoon. Now, he was flying Cobra gunships as the platoon commander of the Raiders. The Cobra was a game changer, outfitted with 17-pound rockets, miniguns, and a grenade launcher that would fire hundreds of M79 type grenades with devastating effect.

Phil would spend much of that tour flying for the Special Forces, supporting B-36 out of Tay Ninh near the Cambodian border. There, three battalions of Cambodians of the 3-D Mobile Strike Force fought the enemy under the leadership of COL Ola Lee Mize, a Medal of Honor winner during the Korean War decades earlier as an enlisted man.

True to form, Phil showed his unmatched dedication, coupled with flying skills, as he earned several Distinguished Flying Crosses and another Silver Star. Of course, these do not come easy, so another Purple Heart was part of the equation, as his Cobra was shot down several times.

Unlike our first tour, Phil and I would only see each other occasionally at our little 145 Club after long days of flying and shooting. Now, at our annual gatherings, we affectionately refer to Phil as our reverse Ace!

TOP—A FLIGHT OF "SLICKS" FROM THE 190TH ASSAULT HELICOPTER COMPANY RETURNING TO BIEN HOA AIR BASE AFTER A MISSION
BOTTOM—LOADING US TROOPS FOR COMBAT ASSAULT WITH 68TH AHC 1969

TOP— PHOTO TAKEN FROM OUR GUNSHIP OF A PRISONER EXCHANGE IN III CORPS SOUTH VIETNAM.
BOTTOM—190TH AWARD PRESENTATION WITH 145TH CAB COMMANDER LTC SELESKAR, AND A VIETNAMESE COLONEL

H MODEL HUEYS

CPT'S HUN AND MCBRIDE REUNITED IN VIETNAM AS CHOPPER PILOT PLATOON LEADERS AFTER HAVING SERVED TOGETHER IN THE SPECIAL FORCES

FLYING "GUNS" AS GLADIATOR 6 IN THE 190TH AHC

RUINING "CHARLIE'S"DAY WHILE HELPING US TROOPS ON THE GROUND

ASSISTING US TROOPS WITH 2.75 ROCKETS FROM B MODEL HUEY GUNSHIP—JAN 1970

TOP—COVERING PRISONER EXCHANGE III CORPS SOUTH VIETNAM
BOTTOM—SUPPORTING 9TH INFANTRY TROOPS FROM CHOPPER
IN DELTA –1970

TOP—US JETS PARKED AT BIEN HOA AIR BASE
BOTTOM—SHOT DOWN HUEY FROM THE 190TH AHC BEING EVACUATED

TOP—HUEY FORMATION— 68TH AHC COMPANY
BOTTOM—OFF ON A MISSION WITH THE 190TH AHC

FLYING WITH THE COBRA JOCKS

While exhilaration is very much a part of flying attack helicopters, risk of injury and death are constant companions. Early spring of 1970, we were supporting the US 9th Infantry Division flying at particularly low levels. Brothers George and Fred Mattingly, two of our stellar crew chiefs, were busting reinforced enemy bunkers from the rear of two separate B Model Hueys. As George was using an M79 grenade launcher to force the enemy out, he was seriously wounded in the throat. The aircraft commander quickly flew him to a nearby field hospital where he was treated and recovered within about a week. Both Mattingly brothers were alive and well a few years ago in Carlyle, PA, where Danney Pickard brought The Spartans and Gladiators together for our biannual reunion.

My close friend, Rick Sauer, then a captain, was the leader of the Playboys, another Cobra platoon in the 334th AHC. On slow days, he could be found sitting around the round table waiting for a mission. Unlike us in the Gladiator platoon, who escorted our Slicks on daily combat missions, they had only gunships, hence, some boring days on standby waiting for something to pop.

Every aviator thinks he is the best pilot in the world! They will not hesitate to inform anyone bored enough to listen. So it was with Rick and I. As a lieutenant, he had been in the infantry as a platoon leader. He had fought at Dak To with the 4th Infantry Division and made an unscheduled exit from that hellhole after taking five rounds in the leg from an AK-47 in November of '67.

Coming back after a day of flying, we would pass by the 334th guys, still waiting for a mission, and chide them about getting a real job. Through the friendly banter, Rick got to calling me "Half Gun," referring to our B Model gunships as merely Slicks with some extra armament. As the Cobras typically started their gun runs about a thousand feet above us, we referred to them as "Nosebleed Specials."

One day, Rick invited me to fly his front seat in a "real gunship." While I was not rated in the Cobra, I was familiar with its armaments and had already logged about 500 hours of combat flying. We went for a trial run, where he further explained the weapons systems and controls in the Cobra. He let me fly the aircraft, which was no small task, given that the collective on the left side and the cyclic on the right were both only about nine inches long in length.

I wondered how I would land the aircraft if Rick could not. We made a couple of practice runs that turned out well. That done, we went to the club to imbibe and listen to, "There I was at 500 feet" stories from guys who had done something that day.

A week later, having a day off, I agreed to fly his front seat. We waited at the Round Table as the knights of lore had done, prior to saving damsels in distress. We waited and we waited until several decks of cards had been worn out. I had to be careful with my comments, as out of the four of us, I was the only Gladiator. The other three pilots were Playboy Cobra Jocks.

My smiles told them everything I was thinking, particularly after several false alarms, but still there was no action. As we turned the mission over to the night shift and headed to the club, the sirens blew. So much for drinks that night as we scrambled to our awaiting pair of Cobras.

The crew chiefs were prepping the two birds as we arrived. The rotor blades were unhooked from the tail booms as we climbed aboard, putting our helmets on, and placing our armor-plated vests over our chests. Affectionately known as "chicken plates," these were worn when we knew we were happily flying into the crap.

The tower gave us our clearance and off we were. Sitting in the front seat of the Cobra, as the radio crackled, I double-checked the armament system. Rick had the thirty-eight—seventeen-pound rockets, while I had the turret with the minigun and the belt-fed 40mm grenade launcher. The Cobra did indeed "bring the max." It was to be an interesting night, where outnumbered US troops would live, and the enemy would die. We would also survive, though barely.

Heading northwest out of Bien Hoa at around 1,000 feet, we soon came upon an American rifle platoon engaged in the nautical twilight. As the orange tracers of our side were going out, the green tracers of the NVA were going in, along with RPGs exploding near the good guys. We spoke to the lieutenant in charge who, from the rasp in his voice, sounded quite shaken.

Rick asked him to throw a smoke grenade toward the incoming fire. We identified the red smoke and came in hot. I fired the minigun while Rick flew parallel to the contact, ensuring that we did not overfly the friendlies. Our wingman followed with rockets a bit further out, and I switched to the 40mm grenade launcher. Through the explosions, we could clearly see dozens of NVA blowing up while making their post haste exit in the relatively light vegetation.

Checking in with the platoon leader, we asked, "How is it now?" He seemed surprised; his voice had changed to a regular tone, stating there was no more incoming. As they were dug in, they did not suffer any casualties, so we said goodbye and told him to call if the enemy returned, knowing they would not. Just to make sure, we made another run with a few rockets on their withdrawal route.

Thinking our work was done, we started for home and that long awaited beer when the radio crackled again. A company of South Vietnamese troops were heavily engaged near a fire support base about twenty minutes to our north. Still having plenty of rockets and grenades, we went directly to the fight. Arriving in the pitch-dark, where the heavy jungle coupled mountainous terrain, it made identifying the combatants much more difficult.

Speaking with the US advisors on the ground with the ARVN, we were able to determine the location of the enemy and started our attack. During our second gun run, as Rick was punching off rockets, illuminating the terrain, I noticed that there was high ground on both sides of the aircraft. I called for Rick to pull up! When he responded with, "What?" I grabbed the cyclic. Rick felt the pressure and pulled the aircraft out of the steep dive. As we climbed, I could see high ground all around us.

Meanwhile, my buddy in the back seat still had his finger on the trigger, lobbing rockets near a village and the fire support base. Since we happened to be in a valley, we did not die that day as did so many others who flew at night in Vietnam. Oh yes, we also heard from the friendly fire base who asked that the helicopter lobbing rockets towards them to stop.

One would think we had enough adventure for one night, but that was not the case. It appeared that my Cobra Jock buddy might have been a bit shaken by the foregoing events. He was on the controls, taking us home 180 degrees in the wrong direction until the long-suffering warrant officer, flying our wing, gave us the proper azimuth.

Finally, as we arrived at the 145th CAB, we came in high and hot, missing the landing area while managing to scatter the maintenance guys working on the flight line. As we used to say back in the day, "If am lying, I am flying." Rick, and his wife, Lynn, remained our good friends for many years, and we saw them often. He completed 20 years in the army, retiring as a lieutenant colonel. Yes, you guessed it. He went to fly for the airlines out of Colorado where he still resides.

. . .

Spring was passing quickly, if there is such a thing in a war zone, and in early April, I flew to Hawaii on R&R to hang out with wifey-to-be, Brenda. I rented a motorcycle on which we covered most of the island of Oahu. It is interesting how flying choppers and riding a Harley share similarity. Both arms and legs are engaged, as are sight and other senses. One feels the wind, and of course, there is the sound that draws you closer to where you belong. That week really went fast, and then it was back to the war.

I flew with Chief Warrant Officers Higgins, Blessum and Monroe along with Captains Phil Spain and Paul Bloomberg among others. Paul and I would take short side trips and let the crew chief and gunner hone their skills shooting a wild deer or two. We would bring them into the chopper and back to the mess hall where our cooks would dress and bake them into excellent meals.

In May, President Nixon ordered the Cambodian invasion. We took a heavy fire team of three B Models to Tay Ninh, close to the border, and stayed for a week. On day one of the invasion, allied tanks and armored personnel carriers were lined up, from The Delta to Northwestern III Corps, as far as the eye could see. When they rolled, the enemy had no chance to get away and tens of thousands of them were killed or surrendered.

A typical day began at first light around 7:00 a.m. We would take the ten-minute flight into Cambodia—shoot, rearm, and shoot again for much of the day in support of US or South Vietnamese troops in contact with the enemy. The operation was a complete success as tons of equipment was abandoned by the retreating VC and NVA. Anyone who wanted an AK-47, or several, could have them. It was a good way to end that tour, having dealt a major blow to an enemy that had not expected us to draw upon the WWII's armor playbook and totally kick their asses.

AH-1 COBRA GUNSHIP
(courtesy of Phil Bodine)

"Awesome aircraft! This was my last one (wife's name LINDA on the nose.) It had the mini-gun and the 40 MM in the turret, 21 rockets on the wings, and the 20 MM.

"The early Cobras had problems with heat due to enclosed cockpit and poor airflow. The newer Cobras came equipped with air conditioning. I had the RAIDERS for my year there, 2nd platoon of the 334th. Great tour and flying the Cobra beat the hell out of walking over the RVN." **—Phil Bodine**

BACK IN THE WORLD

Returning from Vietnam in the summer of 1970, I spent my two-week leave visiting family and friends in Cleveland, Ohio. Then it was off to Fort Benning, Georgia to attend The Infantry Officers Advanced Course, along with about one thousand other captains, most of whom were just back from the war.

Some of the younger captains, who had not yet experienced combat, were exposed vicariously to war in Infantry Hall. After classes, they would suffer *ad nauseum* through war stories told and retold at the "O" club. It was good to reunite with guys with whom we had shared searing times. Phil Bodine and Rick Sauer were there, along with Jerry Cecil, who had won the Distinguished Service Cross at Dak To with the 173rd.

CPT Roger Donlon, who won the Medal of Honor while in Special Forces, drew a lot of attention with his tall statured, physical and emotional presence. Such is still the case at the annual Special Operations reunions in Las Vegas.

As the war in Southeast Asia was winding down, the army was substantially reducing the force. Part of this took the form of terminating officers through a RIF program. The most vulnerable were the Combat Arms, which were the most built up for the war. If one had a reserve commission, as most OCS guys did, with no college degree, chances of getting "riffed" was about ninety percent.

The RIF notices from Infantry Branch had a pink slip that was visible in the mail slots of the captains so affected. Between 1970 and 1975, we would lose tens of thousands of captains to this process.

They were each given about $13,000 and their walking papers. Some left minus an eye, others on one leg or with one arm.

Being in this highly vulnerable group with ten years of service, I put in for an army funded college program and was promptly turned down. The substandard efficiency report rendered when I left the 68th AHC played a major role. The army was looking to retain only quality, and a substandard OER as an aviation platoon leader in combat did not reflect that.

Unwilling to accept what I considered an injustice, I flew up to Washington to address the issue. Walking into Infantry Branch in my summer khakis, I was met by LTC Lehardy, who, after reviewing my file, informed me that this one is close, and I would have to go see the boss. After a short period, I entered the office of the "Boss," who was intently reviewing my file. After saluting, LTC Michael J. Conrad graciously offered me a seat. Looking up from his work, he stated, "Your smile is disarming," and asked if we had met before. I replied, "Yes, sir! You gave me my first Article 15 back at Fort Bragg in 1961."

Smiling, he told me I was doing well now, and rose to shake my hand. As we walked out, he told LTC Lehardy to "take care of this fine young officer." I would meet this great leader again several times down the road, at West Point, among other places.

Now having the halo effect of having been selected for degree completion, the Infantry Advanced Course was a breeze. Brenda finished teaching and came up from Annapolis, Maryland, and we were married in Phoenix City, Alabama. After a weekend honeymoon in Atlanta, it was back to Benning for classes, racquetball, and war stories around Infantry Hall until graduation in July. As classes at the University of Nebraska, Omaha did not start until September, I asked for, and got, a job flying fixed-wing aircraft at Davison Army Airfield that served Fort Benning. Life was good!

Arriving in Omaha in August with my new bride, Brenda and I settled in a new apartment a few miles from the university in the summer of '71. I had been taking college courses at Fort Bragg as an enlisted man for five years, so I only needed one full year to get my degree in criminal justice.

There was plenty of time for leisure activities. I played on the university football team, studied karate, and we took several skiing trips to Colorado. As spring came, we took fishing trips to Minnesota. Before graduating, I busied myself taking fixed-wing flying lessons from a fellow "bootstrapper," who had flown L-19 forward air-control aircraft of the type that saved us at Chi Linh. We reminisced about the war, and I was able to solo in about a week.

...

With the war now seemingly behind us, Brenda and I were blessed by the birth of our two children. Daughter, Tara, was born in October 1973 in a small hospital in Harrisburg, Virginia. Our son, Nicholas, would join our familial unit at West Point in May of 1977. They would live the lives of "Army brats," being dragged from pillar to post for the next twenty years. They were impacted in different ways, but they did thrive. Now they are medical professionals, both having serious wanderlust.

The army was still downsizing, so finding jobs for captains was challenging. I was selected for ROTC duty at Massanutten Military Academy in Woodstock, Virginia. The two years there were spent teaching military subjects to the live-in cadets, along with three, non-commissioned officers. Much time was spent coaching the kids in marksmanship, rappelling, and of course, drill. We also sponsored a ski club and a karate club that was extremely popular with the post-graduates for conditioning. These young men were brought there for a year of football, prior to going to various colleges and universities on athletic scholarships.

During the summer months, when the cadets went home, I would fulfill my requirement to maintain my aviation skills as an army helicopter pilot. Driving two hours, I would stay in the BOQ at

Fort Belvoir, Virginia and fly choppers out of Davison Army Airfield, adjacent to the post. These missions would include flying in and out of the White House about twenty miles away. To ensure I retained the skills for these sensitive missions, I completed a six-week instrument training course, which greatly facilitated flying at night and busting clouds in bad weather.

One evening, on a White House mission, I was conducting the preflight inspection of my Huey. Who shows up to fly with me but my first instructor pilot at Fort Wolters, Texas, CW2 Dave McAdams. Dave and I had both flown in Nam and had not seen each other in five years but reconnected immediately. The mission took us well past midnight as both darkness and weather set in while heading back to the airfield.

Dave was flying as the weather worsened. Our approach to the airfield was under instrument flight rules deep in the dark clouds. As the flight became bumpy, I informed Dave that I was on the instruments. I noticed his nervousness, so I then asked him if I could fly the aircraft. As he had not flown IFR in a while, and I had recently completed intensive instrument training, he seemed relieved when I took the controls.

After about fifteen minutes in the clouds, we came out at minimums and made a smooth touchdown. As we parked the aircraft, he stated, "I knew I made the right decision about you," referring to when he was my instructor and passed me on to the next level, and ultimately to my aviator wings. All of you pilots of generations past and present certainly understand.

. . .

While the Infantry Branch was well overstrength in 1974 because of the buildup for Vietnam, there was a shortage of military police captains and majors. The Military Police Corps solicited branch transfers of officers they deemed fit for police work. I soon received my letter, and after talking with a very impressive military police officer in the

MP Branch, I signed the letter and put on my cross pistols. It all made sense. I had completed MP school at Fort Gordon, Georgia as an enlisted man in '61, and I had my degree in criminal justice and law enforcement. After completing a six-week transition course studying law enforcement and corrections at Fort McClellan, Alabama, I received my orders for Fort Hood, Texas to the 720th MP battalion. There, I had the honor to work with some of the finest soldiers in the army as the commander of the 411th MP company for eighteen months.

The two years at Fort Hood brought selection to major as I was lifted to field grade status on the shoulders of the 411th MP company. 1SG Bobby Brown, also a Green Beret in Nam, was our "Top." He was a coach and counselor to our young soldiers while still enforcing high standards of conduct and performance.

During the first two months, we administered a dozen Articles 15, nonjudicial punishment for minor infractions. The ensuing sixteen months of my command brought only one. Good soldiers will be compliant if they understand the rules.

Our company was later deployed to Fort Chaffee, Arkansas in the spring of '75 when Vietnam fell. Our MPs provided security and law enforcement for the post during the relocation of tens of thousands of Vietnamese refugees who had escaped the communist takeover of their homeland.

Back from Chaffee, the 411th MP company was nominated for The Jeremiah Holland Award, which designates the best military police company in the army. Unfortunately, we came in second to the 82nd Airborne Division MP company of paratroopers at Fort Bragg, North Carolina. Still, it was a great run! Our 411th MPs are still together as civilians, thanks to the efforts of Michael Judd, William P Lamb, Pat Duckett, and Ron Morin, among others who have kept our stellar group of patriots connected in benevolent camaraderie.

...

COL Mcfarland eventually replaced COL Nipper as 720th battalion commander, who went to the US Military Academy at West Point as the provost marshal. I was assigned to the battalion staff as the operations officer. CPT John Bradford, a native Texan, and also a Green Beret, took command of the 411th MP company in 1975, taking it to even higher levels of achievement.

COL Nipper called, as he needed a deputy at West Point. I happily accepted, and in January of 1977, we left Fort Hood and the 720th MP battalion for Wheeling, West Virginia, our "home away from home," to visit with family while on leave.

Leah, my wife's sister, had married Pete Newmeyer, a businessman, entrepreneur, and a singularly outstanding human being in 1960. They were exceedingly kind to our family through the years, and our grown children and theirs are still close to this very day. Sadly, Leah and Pete have passed, but their memories remain strong in our hearts.

TOP LEFT—WITH WIFE TO BE BRENDA VISITING AT FORT WOLTERS, TEXAS DURING HELICOPTER FLIGHT SCHOOL
TOP RIGHT—DRIVING HOME AFTER A DAY OF FLYING AT FORT WOLTERS
BOTTOM—RELAXING WITH WIFE BRENDA DURING THE
INFANTRY ADVANCE COURSE AT FORT BENNING GEORGIA—1970

1LT NICK HUN, CO E, 5TH BN, 2ND BDE RECEIVES BRONZE STAR WITH "V" DEVICE FOR VALOR AGAINST HOSTILE FORCES IN VIETNAM FROM COL JAMES R. YOUNG AT FORT LEWIS, WASHINGTION ON 26 JAN 1968

THE 411TH MP COMPANY

By Michael L. Jewell

Colonel Hun, my commander at the 411th, asked me to write about my experiences as a military policeman while stationed there. I have written two chapters: the first covering my time at Fort Hood, and the second at Fort Chaffee during Operation New Arrivals—MLJ

Texas! Just the sound of the word conjures up fond memories of the Old West. As an aficionado of early black-and-white cowboy movies, I never dreamed that I'd be able to visit Texas, let alone live there.

At eighteen, I had rarely traveled farther from my home than an occasional trip to the big museums and the zoo in Chicago. At almost a thousand miles away, The Lone Star State seemed to be out of reach from my well-ordered life in Benton Harbor, Michigan.

My local army recruiter had posted an offer guaranteeing sixteen months at Fort Hood, Texas in exchange for a three-year enlistment in the US Army as a military policeman. Being one of the largest military bases in the world, Fort Hood was purported to be one-quarter the size of the State of Rhode Island. Fresh out of high school and interested in a career in law enforcement, I jumped at the challenge and signed up in December of 1972. I took my Basic Training at Fort Knox, Kentucky, and Military Police School at Fort Gordon, Georgia from January through May of the following year.

After a fifteen-day leave to catch my breath, I set out for Texas on a Greyhound bus from the terminal in downtown Benton Harbor. Approximately twenty-five hours later, I was southbound on a lonely stretch of Interstate 35, somewhere between Dallas and my destination of Fort Hood.

Arriving at the terminal in Killeen, a typical GI town outside the east gate, I quickly boarded the town transit bus that regularly made its monotonous circuit about the post.

It was still dark when I arrived in front of a white wooden building with dark green trim. A sign painted "John Deere" green with yellow lettering (official colors of the Military Police Corps) identified it as the home of the 411th Military Police Company.

The door to the operations office was open so I walked in, leaving my duffle bag and other accoutrements piled outside in a heap. The first person I was to meet was the CQ runner. He proved to be quite amiable, though I can only remember that he was from Westland, Michigan and had at one time been in Officer's Candidate School. Being from Michigan, we both hit it off right away and soon, he had me temporarily settled in a room used for storage in one of the barracks.

Cluttered with dismantled beds, desks, and chairs, I made my way around the room with some difficulty, but I didn't care. Slightly bewildered and weary from my long ride, I quickly bedded down on one of the mattresses and fell asleep.

The next thing I recall was the bright sunlight shining through the window and seeing SFC Jennings and LT Haller standing in front of it. We were surprised to see each other and I, not long out of training, jumped to attention and saluted.

LT Haller wanted to know who I was and why I was there. I suppose he thought I might be a refugee from another unit, sleeping off a previous night's drinking party. A sober explanation soon cleared the matter and SFC Jennings, who eventually became my new platoon sergeant, assigned me to a room in the second platoon barracks. I inconspicuously settled in.

I liked SFC Jennings and we got along well, perhaps because he was from Port Huron, Michigan. From time to time, SFC Jennings would ask my good friend, Greg Trotter, and I to "police up" the platoon area in advance of an inspection. We figured he came to us because we always cheerfully complied, even when he reluctantly woke us up after pulling a long, weary night on patrol. We never gave him any "guff" like some of the case-hardened draftees who were only biding their time, waiting to get out of the army and go home.

I had joined the military police, first inspired by my father, Burton Z. Jewell Jr., who had served as a MP with the 8450th at Sandia Base, New Mexico, near Albuquerque, back in the 1940s. I came from a "cop" family back home, so my expectations were high, and I looked forward to my first day on patrol in a squad car. I was, therefore, surprised at the things I was to experience in the months after my arrival. Little did I know that I was about to discover what happens when "short time" draftees collide with enlistees of the new volunteer army.

Evidently, our battalion was only expecting one new graduate from the MP school at Fort Gordon, Georgia, who I believe was Gary Moss from Wisconsin. Then I show up without warning. News soon got around about me, and it was suggested that I might be an undercover narcotics officer working for MPI. There was a lot of paranoia in the 411th in those days, and I soon became one of the most distrusted men in the company.

One day, I was confronted by a senior sergeant who angrily demanded that I formally identify myself as an MPI agent. He gave me a hard time, and many of his accusations were merely distortions of things I had innocently said in casual conversation with the other men.

I was not MPI (Military Police Investigator), by the way; only a regular soldier who had dreams of going into the Michigan State Police one day. Fed up with it all, I told that sergeant that if he wanted to question me any further about such nonsense, he had better read me my rights.

One morning, down at the motor pool after pulling a night shift, I was parking my patrol jeep when one of the mechanics came out and began to harass me. He took sadistic pleasure in making me park and repark my jeep until it met with his approval. Finally, having enough of his tomfoolery, I spoke something under my breath and shut off the engine.

As I endeavored to dismount, the mechanic sucker punched me in the face. I never felt it! Slamming him up against the hood of another jeep, I split his lip and tore the shirt off his back. The man in charge ordered me off the premises, and as I walked back to the company area, I was sure my brief army career was over.

The next morning, the motor pool lieutenant came and got me so I could report to the company commander to answer for what I had done. I didn't have a mark on me, but the other guy with whom I fought was there and had a badly swollen face. This didn't help my case any.

I spoke my piece to the commander, and then the mechanic spoke (as well as he could). I had pictured myself spending a year in the Fort Hood stockade, or worse—Fort Leavenworth.

The commander, with more wisdom than I had initially given him credit, simply warned me that he wouldn't tolerate his MPs beating up on mechanics at the motor pool. He then barked, "Get out of my office!"

I suffered even further humiliations as my personal belongings were rifled through when I wasn't in my room. Threatened with being tossed off the balcony or down the stairs, I awoke one morning with a real pig's foot on my pillow. I tried to imagine what kind of person would go to the trouble of procuring a "pig's trotter," just to torment a fellow soldier.

Once, I was cornered in a dark hallway by one of the bigger men in our unit and threatened with a beating. I finally had enough and told him he'd better kill me because he would never get another night's sleep as long as I was alive. I promised to beat him to death with my nightstick when he least expected it.

We stared each other down for several moments, and then he grinned. "Jewell," he said, "You're all right!" We eventually became friends, and I was even invited to his wedding at Lake Travis in Austin.

For a time, I worked the desk at the PMO (provost marshal's office), which is essentially the same as the police station in civilian life. I worked some as a journal clerk, blotter clerk, radio dispatcher, and teletype operator. I also was responsible for checking the paperwork brought in by the road-duty MPs to ensure all the pertinent information was there. Later, I was certified to operate the GCI (Gas Chromatograph Intoximeter), which is a fancy name for a type of breathalyzer.

One day, the enforcement officer, CPT Norbert Kenyon, came up on the MP desk to see what was going on and he saw me. CPT Kenyon didn't like me for some reason, and I seemed to elicit a negative reaction from him every time he saw me. Well, I was buzzing around the MP desk, trying to get my work done, and the phone rang several times. He advised me forthwith, that from now on, the phone would be answered on the first ring. Just then, it rang again, and then again. I stared into the captain's face as if I was frozen. I won't repeat what he said to me, but it wasn't inspiring to say the least.

Several weeks or months later, I received a teletype message from the Temple Texas Police Department informing us of the death of a soldier from a tragic accident. Per army SOP, I was to immediately advise a commissioned officer of the death. Just then, CPT Kenyon walked up on the MP desk. I must have been crazy because any interaction between him and I never seemed to end well.

"Sir!" I said "Per army SOP, I would like to advise you of the death of a Fort Hood soldier that took place in the City of Temple, et cetera, et cetera." I waited for some kind of scathing response, but all he did was stand there and grin from ear to ear. "Jewell," he finally said, "You aren't much for military appearance or bearing, but you sure do have your stuff together!"

I couldn't have been more pleased with his response because, even though it was a bit harsh, I knew he genuinely meant it.

As the weeks and months went by, more and more of the "old guys," as we called them, mustered out and the company filled up with new volunteers. Since nobody had been busted for drugs, most of those old veteran draftees finally realized they had been mistaken about me, and things settled back into a lull. I was also becoming more senior as time passed, and this served to make me invisible.

I noticed there were several guys walking around the company with injuries. One man had been hurt when he flipped a six-wheel, all-terrain vehicle called a Gama Goat. Another one of the old timers had been injured when his Deuce and a Half truck turned over while crossing the Pedernales River on the south side of the Johnson Ranch. This is when I learned that our company had been given the honor of providing security for President Lyndon Johnson's funeral earlier that year.

Frank May, a good friend and fellow MP from Michigan, invited me one day to take a jaunt with him to visit President Johnson's grave and the Johnson Ranch in Johnson City, Texas. When we arrived, a Texas DPS officer was stationed there as an honor guard.

There were always things to do and see in Texas, so Frank and I decided to visit the Longhorn Cavern State Park in Burnet where we learned, among other things, that the Confederate Army had manufactured gunpowder there from bat guano. Before leaving the area, we bravely signed on to do a nature hike that was scheduled to take at least two hours. It was an arid, snakey-looking place that was swarming with large, black mosquitos. I recall how we easily jogged the trail in about twenty minutes to keep from being eaten alive.

Later, we visited nearby Buchanan Dam for a memorable Rueben sandwich with a beautiful view of Buchanan Lake. Large cliffs on the north side of the lake looked like a nesting site for Pterodactyls.

An outdoor concert was held one night on Fort Hood, and I was part of the security contingent. The famous Ray Charles was there to entertain. My partner and I were on foot patrol, and though the music was fine and folks seemed to be having a good time, I vividly remember having open soda cans dumped on us from the crowds seated above us in the bleachers. So much for giving respect to law enforcement.

One night, on patrol with my partner, Gary Moss, we came upon an intoxicated man who had been arguing with his girlfriend and began shooting his pistol at random outside the NCO club. One of the bullets skidded across the asphalt and struck our jeep just below where I was seated.

The man fled the scene as we chased him down, stopping him just up the road on Tank Destroyer Boulevard. Drawing our weapons, we ordered him to freeze as we waited for backup. The man kept trying to dismount his vehicle but was so inebriated that he couldn't get out of the door.

Very soon, military police patrols from all over the post were there, and the man was safely apprehended. His smoking .38 revolver was found lying on the floor of his car. Gary and I looked at each other, grateful that we didn't have to use deadly force to defend ourselves.

One of the most interesting and telling experiences I had with the 411th was a month of AWOL Apprehension duty with my partner, Larry Waters, from Philadelphia. Together, we spent a fast-paced four weeks in our Dodge van, picking up prisoners from jails in Texas and Oklahoma. The van was a traditional style police "paddy wagon" with metal bars on the rear windows and a sliding metal door separating the prisoners from the driver and passenger.

We were sent to a new place every day or two, sometimes spending the night in a local motel. I discovered that the civilian police received bounties for every AWOL they could arrest. One officer told me that he made more money each month catching AWOLs than he could earn with his regular police pay.

Some of the prisoners were relieved to see us when we showed up because now, their running was over. Others, more obstinate, were content with doing anything they could not to go back to army life. Those soldiers we did take back were often required to complete their time in service or fulfill a stint in the post stockade. The worst cases would receive dishonorable discharges and be shown the door.

Once I was sent to the Dallas County Jail with SP4 Steve Kierzek from Chicago and another MP to take custody of ten prisoners. It was only March, but our olive-green, full-sized van was not air-conditioned, and it could get as hot as an oven in the Texas sun. Everything was going fine until the last pickup of the day at the Waco Jail. Advised by the jailer that our prisoner was rife with a bad case of body lice, I was careful when I searched him.

Continuing south to Fort Hood, now with eleven prisoners, the "Dallas boys" somehow found out about the Waco man's "affliction." This motivated them to all move to one side of the van while rocking it back and forth in protest. Fearing a flip over on Interstate 35, we ordered the prisoners to divide themselves up equally on each side and to sit still.

Our threats went unheeded, and we dare not open the van lest they overpower us and escape. We finally decided to shut off the ventilation, and it got hot in the back pretty fast. Soon, a staccato of apologies came our way from the men, promising us that they would behave and settle down. The remainder of the journey was uneventful.

On another day, Larry Waters and I were on our way to the Waco Jail and nearby McLennan County Jail to pick up one prisoner from each establishment. Our first man from McLennan County had been classified as a deserter since he had been away for thirteen years. He was a big man of at least three-hundred pounds but peaceful, and we didn't foresee any problems. Larry was my senior, so he said he would stay in the van with the prisoner, and I could get the second man from Waco Jail.

The man I picked up was short and quiet, so I decided not to restrain him. I was young in those days and figured I could run him down like a rabbit if he decided to take off. When I came outside, however, I found Larry standing outside the van with his nightstick in hand, shouting at his prisoner who was still inside.

Apparently, our quiet man suddenly came alive and chose to try an escape by slamming his massive body against the back doors. When he saw me, he immediately sat back down, and our two prisoners had a quiet ride back to Fort Hood.

I was never about purposely humiliating prisoners and didn't necessarily consider AWOLs to be bad people. Some folks, with varying degrees of maturity, reach a point where they feel they can't take it anymore and go home. My job was to bring these soldiers back to face their responsibilities and perhaps, by treating them with a light hand, they might buck up and do the right thing and be better men for it.

Larry and I were sent to Fort Sill, Oklahoma to pick up a young man that I believe turned himself in. We went by aircraft to the Lawton airport and the next morning, took a cab to the Fort Sill stockade.

Our prisoner looked so young, as if he didn't need to shave more than three or four times a week. The Fort Sill MPs gave us a ride to the airport, but before we went in, I stopped our young man for a discussion. I told him I didn't want to shame him by putting handcuffs on him to be paraded through the airport for what would be called today, "the perp walk!" If he would promise me to behave, we could all have a leisurely flight back to Fort Hood. However, if he gave us any problems, he would rue the day. He smiled and made his promise. I even bought him a can of soda and a bag of chips to seal the deal. *Of the troops and for the troops, right?*

One early morning at the Fort Hood AWOL office, we were given a phone tip that an AWOL and his wife had returned to their home in the City of Killeen. After notifying the Killeen Police Department, we surrounded the house and soon gained entry.

Apparently, the couple had been out of town for several weeks, leaving their dog alone with only food and water. As I entered the front door, the smell hit me like a folded newspaper, and everywhere you looked, there were piles of dog feces.

I easily took the man into custody and cuffed him. His wife, however, was not so happy and soon became animated, screaming and yelling at us until the Killeen officer threatened to arrest her for interfering. I was more than glad to get out of there.

Some of the more remote places we visited in Texas were reminiscent of *Tobacco Road,* keeping in mind that this was back in the early 1970s.

This particular day, Larry and I were in a fully-marked, military police squad car instead of the AWOL van. We departed Fort Hood, due west, to a small town on the other side of San Angelo. As I had intimated earlier, springtime in Texas can be hot. Our sedan was air-conditioned, but the tanker truck we were following was filled with crude oil and gave off a cloud of pungent fumes.

Unable to pass the truck on the narrow two-lane road, we decided to pull off for a while to let it get far ahead of us. Eventually, arriving at our destination, we noted that it was out in the middle of nowhere. The brick building was small but had several stories, and a white picket fence surrounded it.

My partner and I walked inside, and though it was a jail, we were surprised that it looked like someone's living room. We could see into the kitchen, and there was a young man wearing an apron, standing at the sink washing dishes. An elderly lady, with white hair and wearing a dress, came out to greet us.

I just knew we were in the wrong place until the lady spoke. "Are you gentlemen here to pick up your prisoner? John's been such a good boy. I'll get my husband," she said as she glanced back at the young soldier standing humbly at the kitchen sink.

A few moments later, an elderly man wearing a small badge came out and shook our hands. He was the sheriff in charge of the jail.

Soon we were on our way, but before we left, the sheriff told us to come and see him after we left the army and he would hire us. To this day, I sometimes wonder if I had dreamed the whole thing.

One of our journeys took us to East Texas. We found the local town police department and told them we were there to pick up a man for AWOL.

"Oh," the lady said, "We don't have him in custody yet, but know where he lives. I'll have a sheriff's deputy meet you and go with you out to get him."

Larry and I had learned to expect anything on our journeys to these small towns, so we followed the directions that led us far out in the country on a dirt road. Clearly marked "**MILITARY POLICE**," we pulled our van off the road and waited.

A half hour or so passed, with the only sign of life being a farmer on a tractor plowing his field. As Larry and I talked, we watched the farmer get closer and closer and finally pull his tractor up in front of our van.

The man looked like he was at least in his seventies, his leather-like face wizened from years of exposure to the hot sun. We got out to speak with him when I noticed a small badge pinned to a strap on his bib overalls that said, "Deputy Sheriff."

The deputy took a seat in our vehicle and directed us to a long road that seemed to end in a dark wood surrounded by a swamp. An old, two-story house, that hadn't seen a coat of paint in many years, stood in the middle of it.

Apparently, the word had quickly leaked out about us, and the young man lit out for the swamp to escape. We thanked the deputy and gave him a copy of the warrant. He assured us that he would catch him and give us a call, but if he was ever caught, I was never made aware of it.

. . .

Military police units were usually separated from other troops on an army post and fraternization was not encouraged. Developing their own separate cultures, MP units in those days sometimes lost sight of their mission and forgot they were part of the whole. This undesirable attitude took hold on some of the members of our company, including myself to a certain extent.

We began to hear scuttlebutt about a new battalion commander being brought in to straighten us out. We were not terribly surprised then, when we soon received a new company commander and first sergeant, both who had served in the Special Forces in Vietnam.

Evidently, the army was determined to make the needed adjustments and brought in some tough, competent leadership to make it happen. Anyway, this was how we interpreted the situation, figuring that we must be pretty bad if it took Green Berets to sort us out.

Some of us balked and "kicked against the pricks" when brought back to reality. I particularly remember one of the sergeants saying, obviously for my particular benefit, "Jewell, you hear that grumbling and griping? That's the sound of the morale rising in the company among our soldiers." At that time, I didn't understand what he meant.

SSG McGill, our desk sergeant at the PMO, had noticed my less than sparkling attitude. Calling me aside, he gave me one of the most blistering "dressings down" I ever received. Actually, he was stern but sincere, never raising his voice. But he did tell me that my bearing and manner was affecting some of the other young soldiers in the company, making it difficult for those in charge to maintain order. What really stung was when he told me, that in their eyes, I was a leader and these fellows looked up to me. By my attitude, I was giving them all permission and excuse to be rebellious.

I was shocked, of course, when I heard this revelation because I was unable to see this in myself. Mentally, I did my best Steve Urkel, *"Did I do that?"* impression and knew I had to turn it around. Thoroughly admonished and on a new path, I set out to fix what was broken.

I soon noticed, that within a few weeks, positive changes began to take place throughout our whole company under the capable leadership of CPT Nick Hun and 1SG Bobby Brown. The 411th Military Police Company soon became refocused and more disciplined.

A certain amount of bellyaching in an army unit is normal and to be expected, but we eventually were "squared away," ready for the responsibilities soon to be put upon us. To this day, I am grateful for the officers and NCOs that took the time to make a difference in my life.

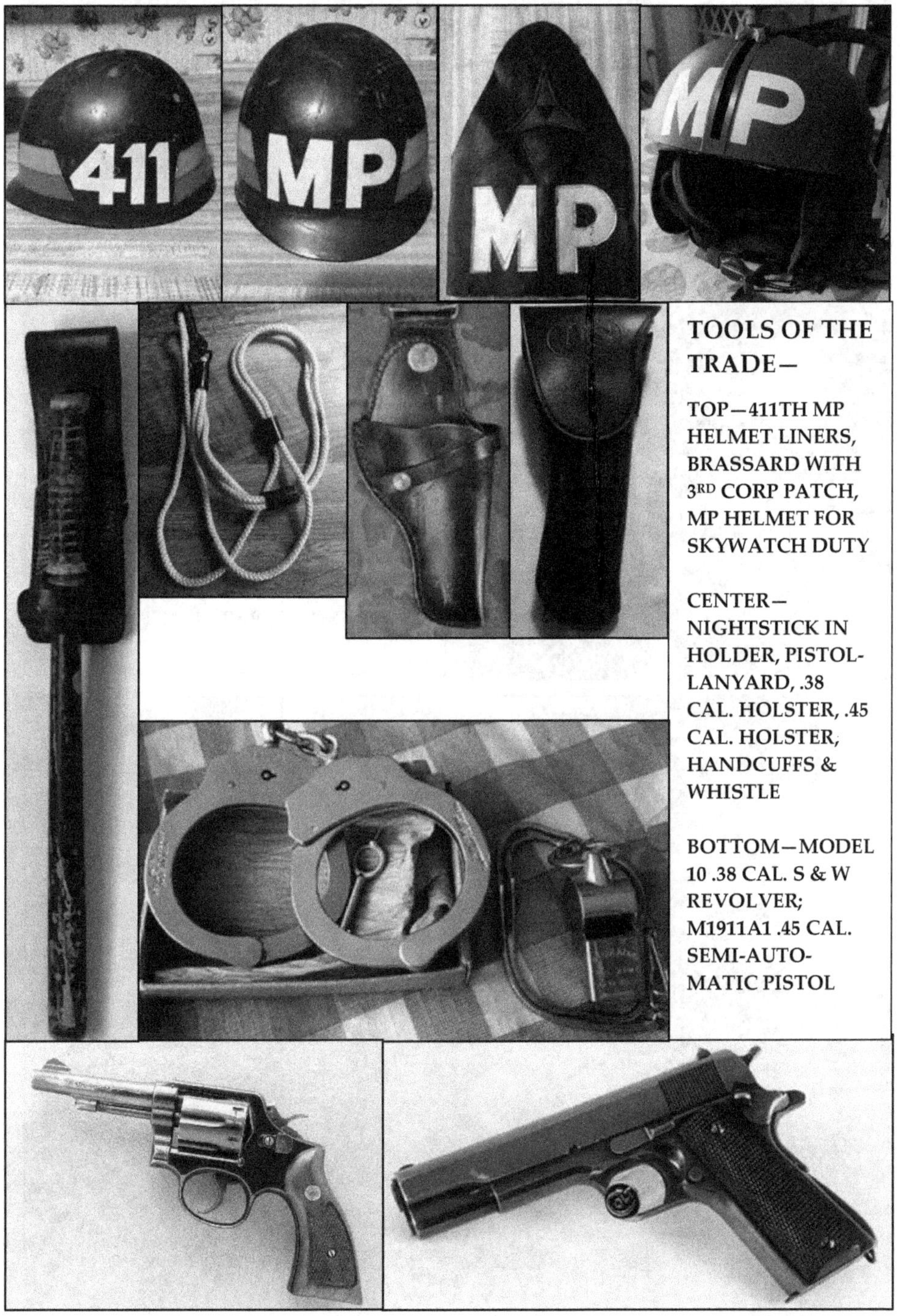

TOOLS OF THE TRADE—

TOP—411TH MP HELMET LINERS, BRASSARD WITH 3RD CORP PATCH, MP HELMET FOR SKYWATCH DUTY

CENTER—NIGHTSTICK IN HOLDER, PISTOL-LANYARD, .38 CAL. HOLSTER, .45 CAL. HOLSTER, HANDCUFFS & WHISTLE

BOTTOM—MODEL 10 .38 CAL. S & W REVOLVER; M1911A1 .45 CAL. SEMI-AUTO-MATIC PISTOL

TOP ROW—JOHN BOOK & WIFE LESLIE

BELOW—L-R: DAVID KEMPAS, PATRICK THALER

GUARD MOUNT IN KHAKIS

TOP LEFT—GREG TROTTER GOING ON TOWN PATROL
TOP RIGHT—THE GUYS GETTING READY TO GO ON POST PATROL
CENTER RIGHT—STEVE HUBER
BOTTOM ROW L-R: ED KLOBUCHIR, MP'S APREHENDING A "10-8"

TOP LEFT—JOHN HOOKER, RON MORIN, JIM COWEN
TOP RIGHT—BARBARA KLEINDIENST
BOTTOM—L-R: ANNE MORRISON-ZAVALA, GARY MOSS

TOP LEFT—UNK MP EARLY PHOTO 1972/ 73 (NOTE THE 5TH ARMY PATCH)
TOP RIGHT— RONALD RODRIGUEZ
BOTTOM PHOTO-FRONT ROW—L-R: ROB HIRT, DAVID BRAGG, MIKE WOOD
BACK ROW—L-R: JIM SQUIRES, GREG TROTTER, RALPH JEFFRIES

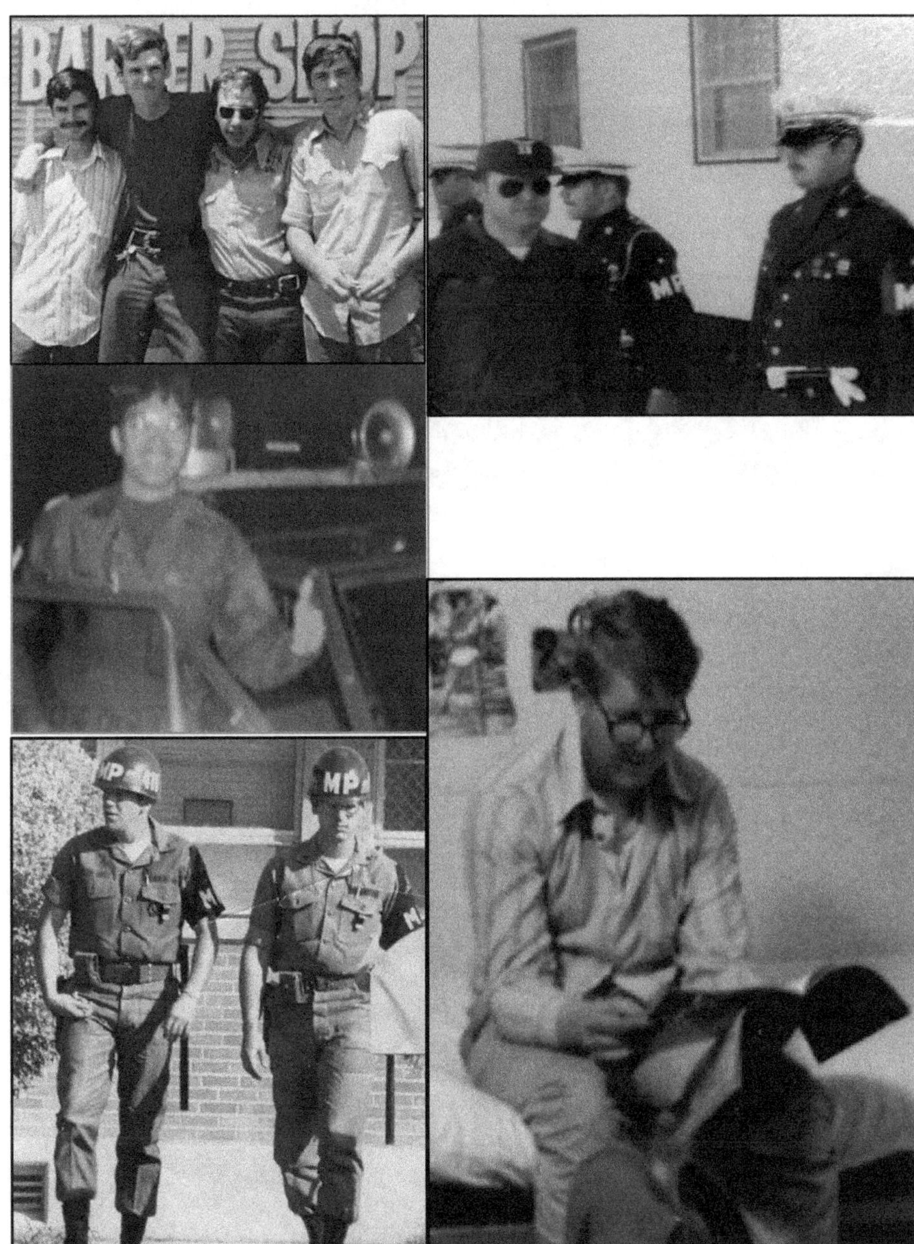

TOP LEFT—L-R: MIKE JUDD, GREG SCHONBERNER, PAUL JUERGEN, RALPH JEFFRIES
TOP RIGHT—CPT HUN GUARD MOUNT INSPECTION
LEFT CENTER—MILTON CHING
BOTTOM LEFT—UNIDENTIFIED MP WITH FRANK MAY (ON RIGHT)
BOTTOM RIGHT—DANNY NORTHERN SEATED ON BUNK

TOP ROW—L-R: DANIEL J. MEANY, STEVE KIERZEK, TED SMITH
BOTTOM—411TH COMPANY GUARD MOUNT
(SSG ROBERT HERRICK STANDING OUT FRONT)

TOP ROW—L-R: DONALD MURPHY, WAYNE SKARKA
BOTTOM—L-R: GREG TROTTER, GREG SCHONBERNER

ASSORTED 411TH PHOTOS; BOTTOM RIGHT—JESSIE AYALA

TOP—GUARD MOUNT
BOTTOM—L-R: RICHARD MANLEY & JOHN OREY WITH A SNAKE SKIN

TOP—L-R: KENNETH SHERMAN; MILLIE ORTIZ (BOTH PHOTOS)
CENTER L-R: 1LT ED WOJTYNA, JOHN OREY, MIKE WOOD
BOTTOM ROW—L-R: 1LT WALLACE REDNER & INSIDE POLICE CAR

TOP– L-R: KATHRYN FISHER-BINGHAM & GEORGIA SUE WARD
BOTTOM–LEO MCCARTHY GETTING READY FOR TRAFFIC POINT DUTY, APRIL 14, 1974, EASTER SUNDAY

TOP—CPT HUN WITH SGT MORIN—GUARD MOUNT INSPECTION BEFORE TOWN PATROL
BELOW—CPT HUN (STANDING) AND LT REDNER SEATED IN JEEP WITH MP GORTON AND MP MESSINA IN BACK SEAT—ORTT

1973 FORD GALAXIES WITH FACTORY INSTALLED CERTIFIED POLICE INTERCEPTER PACKAGE
TOP L-R: ED KLOBUCHIR, MIKE JEWELL,
CENTER: ROBIN LEES, MIKE JEWELL
BOTTOM ROW: BILL VAUGHAN (BOTH PHOTOS)

TOP LEFT—CPT JOHN W. BRADFORD,
TOP RIGHT—MIKE JEWELL W/ X-RAY 27
BOTTOM ROW L-R—KATHY REITZ IN CLASS A'S & FATIGUES

TOP ROW—SGT RON MORIN, MILTON CHING, DAVID KEMPAS
CENTER ROW—CR SINDERUD, LARRY POTTS, MIKE JUDD
BOTTOM ROW—MIKE JEWELL, CPT NICK HUN/ CO OF 411TH MP CO

TOP ROW—L-R: FRANK MAY, ROBIN LEES
BOTTOM ROW—LARRY WATERS, ALLEN HAUSAFUS, BILL JONES

TOP—BREMS BARRACKS, FORT GORDON, GEORGIA, NAMED AFTER PFC PATRICK JOHN BREMS, AN MP WHO WAS KILLED IN VIETNAM WHILE PERFORMING ACTS OF BRAVERY AND HEROISM
BOTTOM—GROUP PHOTO DURING FIELD OPERATIONS

TOP ROW—L-R: STEVE LOWE, LEE RILEY
BOTTOM ROW—TRAFFIC CONTROL DUTY AT PRITCHARD STADIUM
L-R—BARBARA FEILEN-HIRT, MILTON CHING, MARY STEBENNE, JANICE EATON (PHOTO COURTESY OF MILTON CHING)

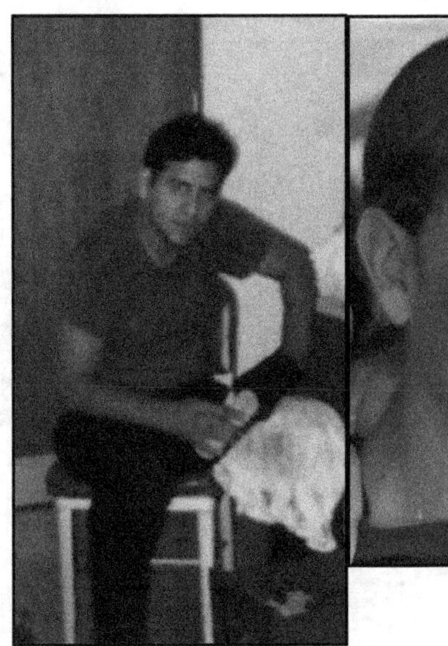

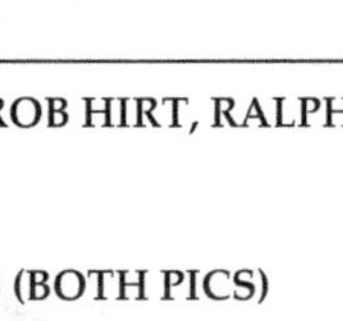

TOP ROW—L-R: PEDRO CAVAZOS, ROB HIRT, RALPH JEFFRIES
RIGHT CENTER—JIM KARL
BOTTOM ROW—ROBERTO SALINAS (BOTH PICS)

TOP—TYPICAL 411TH GUARD MOUNT—SGT SCOTTY MCCARENS (SALUTING). FROM R-L: ROB HIRT, MIKE JEWELL, TOM YENCHIK, TERRY HUNT, WAYNE SKARKA, UNK, JIM COWEN
BOTTOM L-R: LANCE WARD ON GATE DUTY & JOHN M. BECKLING JR & WIFE TAE SUN

COL Christopher Gershel, USA, Retired

August 8, 1942 - July 1, 2020

TOP LEFT—411TH GUYS ON ORTT
TOP RIGHT—COL GERSHEL OBIT
CENTER—L-R: CHRIS MURRAY, DENNIS KUBENKA, JERRY MCKEAN
BOTTOM—L-R: MIKE VERTREES, GARY MOSS, MIKE WOOD

411TH GUARD MOUNT IN KHAKIS

RAY CHARLES

IN CONCERT

PRICHARD STADIUM

8 August 1973

Admission: $1.50 2000 Hours

TOP—SGT RON MORIN PREPARING TO PULL LANYARD TO FIRE OFF MORTAR AT BUILDING #1 (POST HQ) TO SOUND RETREAT
BOTTOM—ANNOUNCEMENT FOR RAY CHARLES CONCERT
411TH MP COMPANY PROVIDED SECURITY FOR THIS EVENT

TOP—PAT DUCKETT— FORT HOOD'S FIRST FEMALE MILITARY POLICE ACCIDENT INVESTIGATOR.
BOTTOM ROW— DAVID R. LOVE

TOP—READY FOR ROUTINE PATROL
BOTTOM—L-R: MP REYNOLDS, ART SHELDON, JOHN KIRBY

TOP—CHRIS MURRAY, TERRY HUNT, PAUL JUERGEN
BOTTOM—RICHARD COPENHAVER

THE 411TH AT FORT CHAFFEE

By Michael L. Jewell

It was April of 1975, and the United States military was extracting all of its forces out of Vietnam. Now, in the absence of any formidable resistance, the NVA had flooded into South Vietnam and was poised at the outskirts of Saigon for the inevitable. Like a mad dog with its dripping jaws around the throat of a tender deer, it would soon be all over for the South Vietnamese people who had been trying desperately to hold onto their country.

As a humanitarian gesture to those who had been our friends, thousands of Vietnamese evacuees were brought to the United States for resettlement. Some went to Camp Pendleton, California, and others to Fort Indiantown Gap, Pennsylvania. A third group was sent to an old army post outside of Fort Smith in Arkansas named Fort Chaffee.

These kinds of operations required the services of the military police, so almost overnight, the 411th MP company and elements of the 401st MP company were uprooted and readied for convoy. There was packing to be done, family members to be settled, shot records updated, and futures to be generally rescheduled.

I had just signed up for an EMT course at Central Texas College, but it was not meant to be. I would be spending that time in deployment with the rest of my company to Fort Chaffee on Operation New Arrivals.

I remember well our military convoy as we passed through town after town in a long line of jeeps, two-and-a-half ton trucks, and other assorted military vehicles. Our MPs were impressive as their jeeps peeled off from the column with precision to block every intersection so we never had to stop for traffic lights or stop signs. When the last vehicle in the convoy passed, the MP jeep blocking traffic would fall in behind, and the next intersection was automatically blocked by the lead MP jeep at the front of the column. Smooth as silk!

We stopped as needed for rest breaks where suitable places could be found. Part of the way it poured down rain, so we wore our raincoats. I remember 1SG Brown doing a belly laugh when he pulled up to a rest stop along the highway, and all of the men in our company were lined up along a fence in their bright yellow raingear to relieve themselves. Later, we stopped at a college in Texarkana to eat supper in their cafeteria. I'm sure we were a sight the students never expected to see.

The first several days at Fort Chaffee were spent getting settled. It was sloppy and wet and rained a lot. I remember my fatigues being constantly damp and I chafed in places I don't want to mention. We ate mostly C-rations until the mess hall could be set up. An old sergeant showed me how to heat my dinner by putting the unopened metal cans on the exhaust manifold of my jeep.

None of the Vietnamese evacuees had yet arrived, so we patrolled the deserted streets among the old pre-WWII barracks. If my memory serves me, there were twenty-four static posts (wooden guard shacks) spaced at intervals up and down the streets of Fort Chaffee. These were to be eventually occupied by military police working twelve-hour shifts. Then, one day, the aircraft began to land, mostly C-141 cargo planes, carrying our charges from Vietnam.

Over twenty-four thousand souls when it was finally over.

When the first Vietnamese evacuees began to disembark at Fort Chaffee, I encountered a few ARVN officers, still in uniform, wearing their insignia of rank. I saluted them just as I had saluted other officers from different branches of our military and foreign countries.

Someone asked me why I was wasting my time saluting officers from a defeated army and country that no longer existed. That was not entirely true, of course. The South Vietnamese troops we left in Vietnam to make their "last stand" against the communists were, at that very moment, fighting for their lives. Brave men were still dying over there.

I have never regretted saluting those officers. They smiled and returned my salutes, grateful for what little honor had been left them. I often wondered what was going through their minds. Perhaps my salutes only made them painfully aware that "all glory was now fleeting."

I didn't know what to expect when I was finally stationed on my first static post. Cautioned about language and conduct by our commander, CPT Hun, I was soon set afloat in a sea of bewildered and frightened faces.

I learned a few Vietnamese words and phrases to get me through, but most of the people spoke English very well. Some even spoke French fluently due to their history with France and their rubber plantations.

A typical day with the evacuees was rarely boring. We "broke starch" and were ready for posting by 0700 hours. There was a lot of foot traffic in the area; perhaps not unlike a typical village in Vietnam. The people would sometimes stop to ask me questions or get directions.

A little boy, about three years old, was brought to me with his eye cut and partially hanging out of the socket. I quickly put a sterile bandage over it and carried him into a nearby first-aid station where a Vietnamese doctor quickly rendered assistance.

There was a lot of truck traffic carrying supplies and the occasional flatbed semitrailer loaded with vegetables and bags of rice. Amongst the confusion, it seemed that nosy intruders were ever attempting to sneak in and get a closer look for themselves. There were also many charitable and humanitarian organizations under the auspices of the State Department to help with all the resettlement issues.

On a night shift, it was not unusual to see a film being projected against the sides of an old barracks as a movie screen. Hundreds of people would sit out on the lawns to watch the entertainment.

Many of the Vietnamese people came to America with their savings in the form of gold coins and bullion. A local bank from Fort Smith set up a trailer on post to convert the gold into cash. This required extra security from the military police.

One morning, after a long, weary night in a dark static post, the sun began to rise. The day would surely prove to be typically hot and humid. I noticed a Vietnamese woman in her late twenties approaching me from the shadows. With a pleading look on her face, she pulled up her dress, and I was shocked to see her baby hanging half out of her, dripping with blood and amniotic fluid. I quickly got on the radio, and soon, a Ford MP sedan arrived and transported her to the hospital. I occasionally wonder what ever happened to that newborn citizen, conceived in South Vietnam and born in the United States of America.

After the Vietnamese and some Cambodians had been in Arkansas for a while, they became homesick and requested to be returned to Vietnam. That is when I added the word *repatriation* to my vocabulary. The American authorities tried to convince them that it would be in their best interests to stay in America, explaining that the current regime might imprison them for their disloyalty, or worse.

Most of these folks wanted to be in the United States and were grateful for the opportunities afforded them. To show their gratitude, and perhaps to convince the shakier ones to stick it out, an elaborate parade with flags and streamers was put on for all to see. However, this did not convince the people who were determined to return home. The army finally repatriated them back to Southeast Asia to face whatever consequences awaited them.

I had heard rumors later on that some, or all, of them had been executed by the communists, which seemed to be par for the course in that part of the world in those days.

Late one evening, I was advised by some of the evacuees that a man had been injured in one of the barracks. Several of us MPs followed these fellows into a dark room where a young man lay bleeding on the floor, close to death. I determined that he was suspected of being a Viet Cong soldier and was stabbed by person or persons unknown with an ice pick.

A very little boy came to my static post one afternoon, apparently lost. I asked several passersby to ask him where he lived so I could reunite him with his people, but no one could understand him. Finally, I found a man who was able to converse with him and tell me where he lived.

"Why couldn't the others understand him," I asked the man. He smiled. "The boy is a Cambodian."

The Vietnamese people had been through much turmoil for countless years, many of them knowing nothing but war. This was evident to me one hot, humid afternoon when an army reserve unit, doing summer training at Fort Chaffee, began firing machine guns at a nearby gunnery range. Suddenly, many of the Vietnamese folks began to shout and scatter. Some just fell to the ground where they stood until we could convince them that it was only a training exercise. I had never witnessed mass fear like this before.

As I have mentioned, the summers in Arkansas along the Oklahoma border were very hot and sultry. A bunch of us from the 411th decided to go to Fort Smith one night and watch the newly released movie, *JAWS*. At least there would be air-conditioning inside the theater.

Unsurprisingly, the movie was intense, and the startled girl seated in front of me splashed her drink in my face when the giant shark burst out of the water!

Later, after eating supper, we all got the bright idea of sneaking into an on-post facility that boasted a well-lighted, Olympic-sized swimming pool. Dressed only in our "unmentionables," we were having a good time when one of the guys decided to swim underneath one of our MPs, Pat Duckett, and bite her on the leg. With the great white shark in the movie still fresh on her mind and a set of teeth around her ankle, her response was predictable. Fortunately, she survived the *faux* shark attack and still laughs about it to this day. As a side note, Pat went on to become Fort Hood's first female military police accident investigator.

Dug in for a while at Fort Chaffee, my life at Fort Hood seemed like a long time ago. I was, therefore, surprised when they ordered me back to attend a trial for a drug bust that I had made several months before. I remember approaching the massive CH-47 Chinook helicopter with its twin rotor blade system already beating the air.

Dubious at first, I remembered seeing a film where the rotors had broken apart on one of these in flight, and it crashed like a hot rock. Biting my lip, I got on board, and one of the crew strapped me in next to the door where I would be able to view the dizzying topography far below.

We made a stop at Love Field in Dallas, and then, in the pitch darkness of night, we proceeded on southward to Fort Hood. I went to the trial the next morning and afterwards, hitched a ride back to Chaffee with a sergeant going that way.

One of the most interesting things I had experienced was being part of a security detail for a VIP's helicopter. Bo Callaway, secretary of the army under Presidents Nixon and Ford, came to Fort Chaffee for an inspection.

My MP partner and I were standing by at Building #1 (Post HQ) when three Huey helicopters flew in from the horizon. I smiled as each of the choppers feigned a landing and then flew away again. Finally, the one transporting the secretary landed. When he and his staff disembarked, my partner and I hopped aboard and the chopper flew us to the other side of the post. We remained with it until the secretary was done with his inspection, and soon he was on his way again. I would have liked to have asked for an autograph, but it wouldn't have been appropriate.

A somewhat tragic thing occurred one late afternoon near the end of our time at Fort Chaffee. A soldier had come to us from an infantry unit to train OJT (on-the-job training) as an MP. We knew little about him except that he had been to Vietnam.

Several of us noticed, that soon after arriving at Chaffee, he began showing signs of anxiety and instability. One evening, he fashioned a long pole and was carrying it around like a spear. If someone approached him, his eyes grew wide and he raised his "spear" in a threatening manner.

SFC Thomas, our platoon sergeant, was summoned and he instinctively knew what was wrong. These were the days when people had only begun talking about soldiers and the effects of combat on them. This man was evidently suffering from some form of PTSD (Post Traumatic Stress Disorder).

SFC Thomas ordered us all back into the barracks and told us to shut the door and stay inside. Immediately, we could hear some loud shouting and physical scuffling. When we dared to look out the door, SFC Thomas was sitting on the steps with his arm around the soldier, comforting him.

Apparently, the man experienced a bad time in Nam, and now, being exposed again to an environment with thousands of Vietnamese walking about set him off. He was taken away for medical attention, and I never saw him again.

On one of the few times I wasn't assigned to a static post, a radio call came out that there was a burglary in progress at the Salvation Army clothing warehouse. Rushing to the scene, I met LT Wallace Redner, who was trying to apprehend the dozens of Vietnamese who had broken in and were running off with armloads of donated clothes. Together, and along with several other MPs, we grabbed and held onto as many of the larcenists as we could.

One man I caught was put in handcuffs, and several days later, I appeared in court to testify against him. The army did not know how to classify the Vietnamese because they were technically not US Citizens. Finally, they decided to call them US Civilians.

The man's defense attorney was Vietnamese, and in happier times, had a practice in Saigon. He questioned me intensely while I was on the stand and skillfully walked me through a thread of logic that became his defense. The attorney reasoned that the Salvation Army's cache of clothing was specifically for the use of the Vietnamese people. Therefore, because his client was Vietnamese, the clothes that he took were technically his, so he couldn't be guilty of stealing his own property.

I was impressed by the lawyer's defense, but evidently, the Arkansas magistrate was not and ordered the defendant to spend thirty days in the county jail.

Another time, I was dispatched to make a report on a larceny, but first, the desk sergeant had me stop by the Special Forces barracks to pick up a Green Beret to act as my interpreter. I was shown into a well-appointed room, occupied by a master sergeant wearing the familiar 5th Special Forces flash on his beret and the arrowhead patch with sword and lightning bolt on his shoulder. He greeted me cordially and asked if my first sergeant was Bobby Brown. When I answered in the affirmative, he told the story behind his nickname, "Claymore Brown." We had heard him called by that name many times, but no one could find out what it meant.

Apparently, when 1SG Brown was in Vietnam, he had chased down an enemy soldier who desperately tried to escape his grip with an outstretched arm. A South Vietnamese soldier who got overly zealous, squeezed the "clacker" that detonated a series of claymore anti-personnel mines. 1SG Brown, who was evidently standing in the sweet spot between the kill zones, was not hurt. However, when the smoke cleared, all that was left was the bloody extended arm of the prisoner that 1SG Brown held firmly by the hand. Hence the nickname—*Claymore Brown!*

I suppose it was inevitable that some of us would make friends with the Vietnamese refugees, though we were advised not to fraternize. Spending twelve hours per day at a static post, it was not unusual to receive visitors of all ages that wanted to talk and hone their English skills. Sometimes, we would see the same people on a daily basis as if we had set appointments.

A lovely young lady, who was several years older than me, would frequently stop by and chat, sometimes handsomely dressed in a colorful *áo dài,* the traditional dress of Vietnamese girls and women. Her father had evidently held an important government post in Saigon. Sadly, her brother was still in Vietnam, fighting to the last man with the South Vietnamese Army, or what was left of it.

I found out that she was about to have a birthday and bought her a card at the PX that had a kitten on the front. She was so surprised and asked me, "How did you know?" I didn't understand at first, until she told me she had been born in the "Year of the Cat," according to the Vietnamese zodiac. Her eyes sparkled with tears as she thought I had purposely chosen that card with a kitten just for her. It was kind of a sweet moment, but I suppose it was serendipity!

Our final day of duty at Chaffee ended when we were relieved by the military police from the Presidio of San Francisco. Soon, I was on my way home to Fort Hood in a car with several other MPs. Our great adventure, which began with much fanfare several months earlier in an official military convoy, ended with hardly a squeak or a notice.

. . .

The 411th Military Police Company thrived under the leadership of CPT Nick Hun, 1SG Bobby Brown, and many other officers and NCOs. This later was made evident when we were rated the second-best military police company in the US Army.

Many of us who served in Operation New Arrivals had never

been to Vietnam or in combat of any kind. However, I believe our value to the war was important and genuine. Had the politics of the day been different, I'm sure we would have, and should have, won the war in Vietnam.

The 411th at Fort Chaffee played an important part in buttoning up the war. Others were there at the beginning. We were there at the very end.

. . .

In January of 1977, President Gerald R. Ford created, by executive order, the Humanitarian Service Medal to be awarded to those who meritoriously participated in a significant military action or operation of a humanitarian nature. The medal was later approved for those who participated in Operation New Arrivals at Fort Chaffee, Arkansas.

I personally applied for the HSM but was advised that the army had no evidence that I had ever been there. Surprised, chagrined, and perhaps feeling a bit unappreciated, I let it go, unable to understand how my service, and the service of a whole company of military police in a major operation, could go unnoticed.

However, many years later with the help of the internet, a few of the men and women from our old unit got together to see if there were any more out there with a similar experience. An investigation by the army and the hard work of a few amazing people, including Michael and Lesa Judd, Judge Joey M. Cobb-AAL, Cassy Fulghum-PA, Michael Patterson-VA District Mgr. of Tupelo, MS, our company commander, Colonel Nick Hun, and US Congressman, Trent Kelly, 1st Dist. of Mississippi, finally revealed the truth. It seems that in the haste of the deployment, our orders did not list us specifically by name but by the total number of persons sent to Fort Chaffee.

Finally approved, the HSM was awarded to those MPs of the 411th who had participated in Operation New Arrivals at Fort

Chaffee, Arkansas. I think I appreciate it more now than if I had received it years ago because it brought our members back together for one last "hurrah!"

My final thought in closing is that the 411th Military Police Company of the 720th Military Police Battalion will always be a large part of my life. I will always love it, and my friends, with whom I proudly served.

TOP—GETTING READY TO LEAVE ON CONVOY FROM FORT HOOD TO FORT CHAFFEE—APRIL 1975

BOTTOM—
TAKING A BREAK ON CONVOY TO FORT CHAFFEE AT TEXARKANA:
1. MIKE JEWELL 2. SGT TYLER 3. ROBIN SCHILICTING-GILES
4. ROGER FLUKE 5. RALPH JEFFRIES 6. ANNE MORRISON-ZAVALA
7. JOSE ZAVALA 8. ERIC GARDNER

TOP LEFT—VIETNAMESE PIASTERS
TOP RIGHT—HSM (HUMANITARIAN SERVICE MEDAL) AWARDED TO THOSE WHO SERVED AT FORT CHAFFEE DURING OPERATION NEW ARRIVALS
CENTER RIGHT—ART VANDYKEN "CHILLING" IN HIS BUNK AT FORT CHAFFEE
BOTTOM LEFT—MP ON GATE DUTY

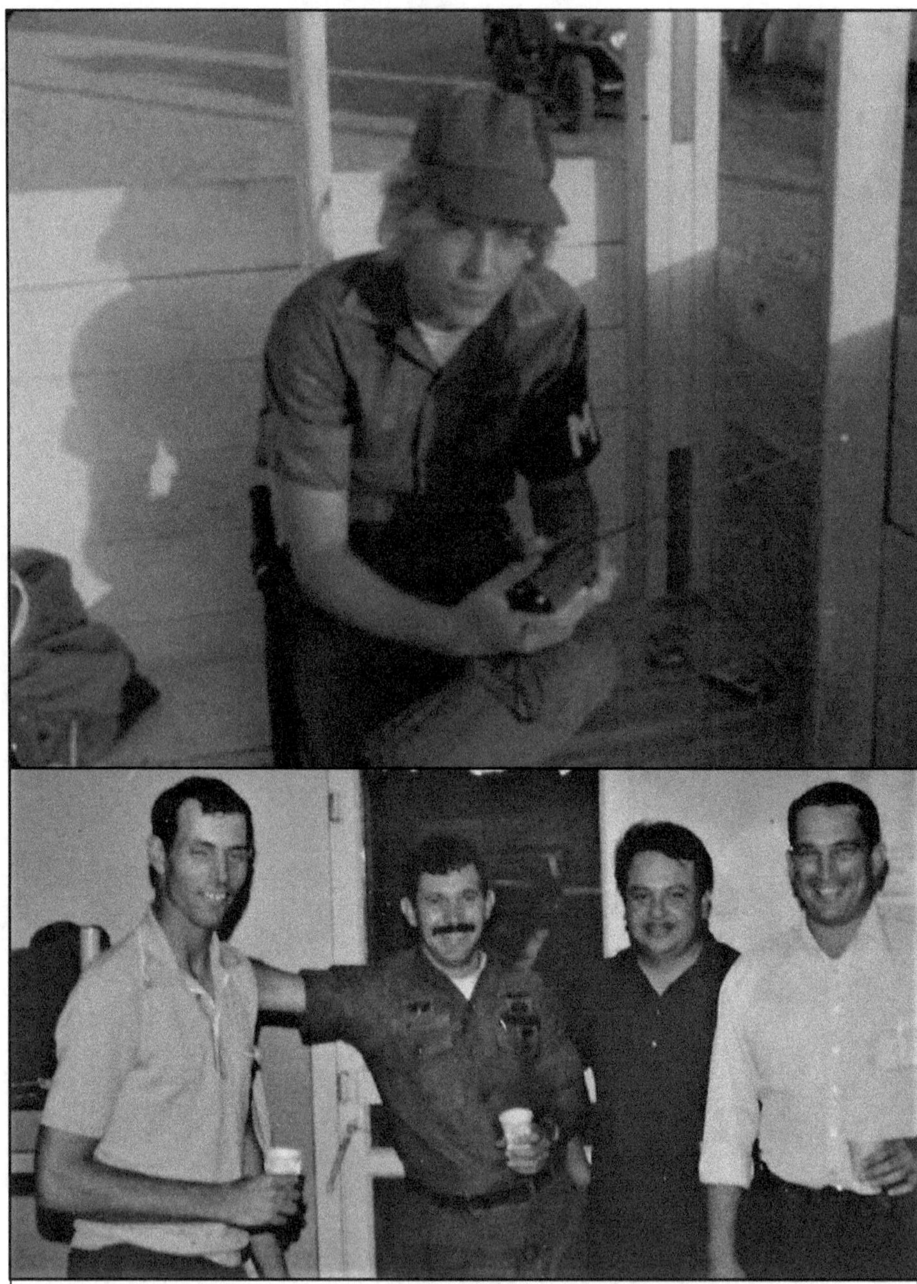

TOP—MARLA LITWIN ON A STATIC POST
BOTTOM—L-R: SFC WALTER THOMAS, 1SG BOBBY BROWN, SSG MARIO JACINTO, SSG TYLER

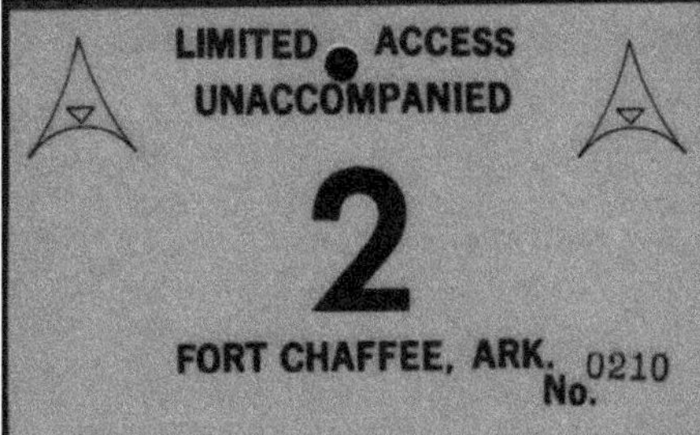

TOP LEFT—EASTER MESSAGE DRAWN BY A VIETNAMESE REFUGEE
TOP RIGHT—RED AUTOMOBILE STICKER FOR PARTICIPANTS AT FORT CHAFFEE; YELLOW BADGE—ONE OF MANY TYPES OF ACCESS BADGES
BOTTOM ROW—L-R: MP FROM PRESIDIO OF SAN FRANCISO & VIETNAMESE CHILDREN; VIETNAMESE BOY

TOP— VIETNAMESE CHILDREN ATTENDING SCHOOL
CENTER LEFT—VIETNAMESE WOMEN WALKING PAST THE POST EXCHANGE
CENTER RIGHT—VIETNAMESE CHILDREN VISITING A STATIC POST
BOTTOM—REFUGEE BILLETS AND STORM CLOUDS ON A SULTRY HOT ARKANSAS DAY
(INSET—LT REDNER SECURING A BARRICADE)

TOP—L-R: MIKE JEWELL AND TED SMITH COMING BACK FROM MESS HALL
BOTTOM—JIM COWEN STANDING BY POLICE CAR (AND INSET PHOTO)

CH-47 CHINOOK HELICOPTER IN THE DISTANCE AGAINST A FORT CHAFFEE SKY

UPON OUR INITIAL ARRIVAL AT FORT CHAFFEE, (THEN) CAPTAIN HUN SPOKE TO US ABOUT DUTY AND WHAT HE EXPECTED OF US REGARDING OUR CONDUCT AMONG THE VIETNAMESE PEOPLE. I WAS HERE AND REMEMBER THIS DISTINCTLY. OUR UNIT WAS BLESSED WITH THIS EXCEPTIONAL LEADER AND COMMANDER—MIKE JEWELL, MAY 1975

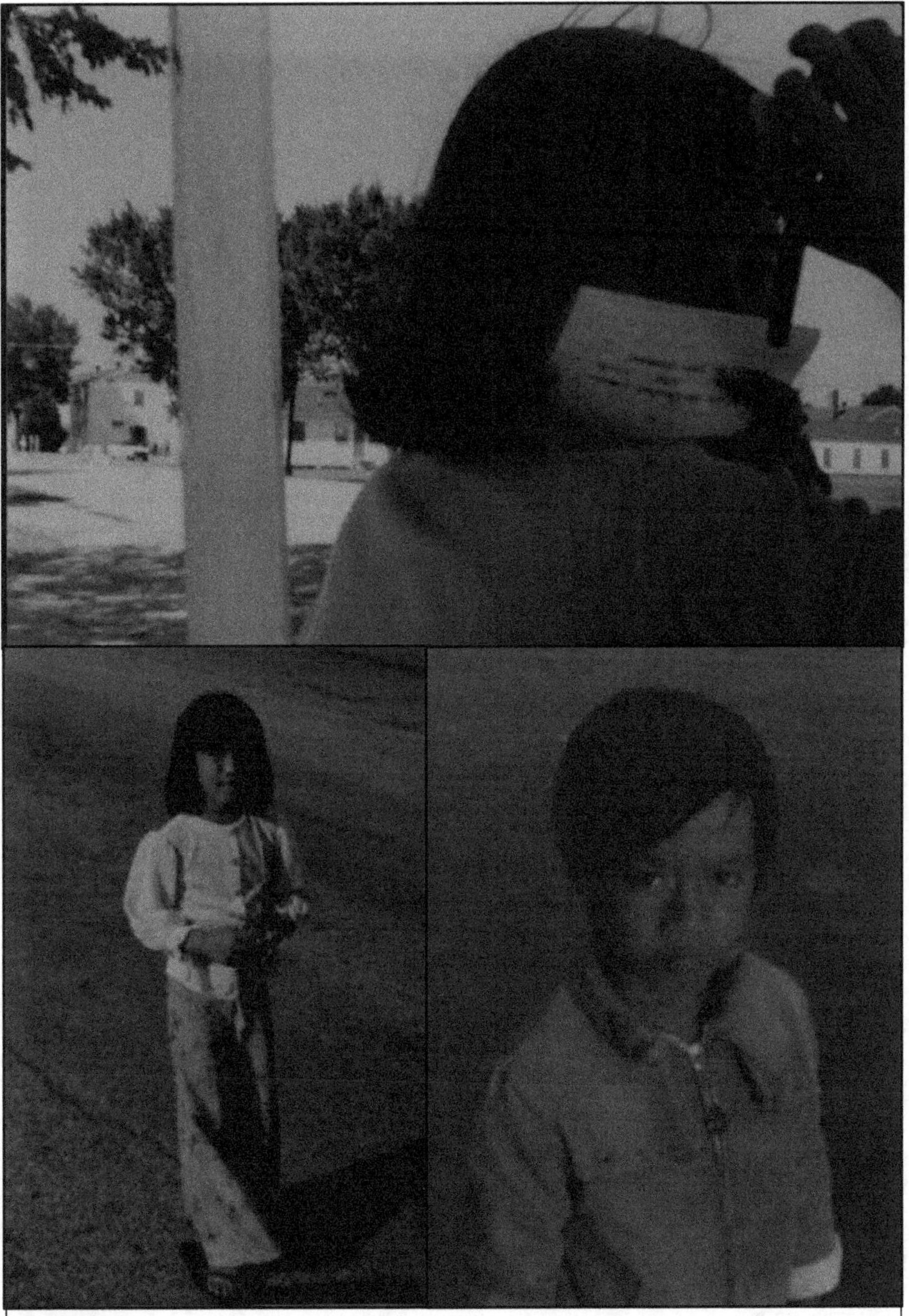

TOP PHOTO— A FRIEND
BOTTOM ROW—VIETNAMESE GIRL & BOY

TOP LEFT—ROBIN SCHLICTING-GILES GUARDING BANK TRAILER
TOP RIGHT— ANNE MORRISON-ZAVALA & PETE CAVOZOS ON STEPS OF BARRACKS
BOTTOM LEFT— DEBBIE LEWIS, LEONARD SCOTT IN FRONT OF FORT CHAFFEE BANK TRAILER
RIGHT CENTER—DAVID KEMPAS ON GATE DUTY

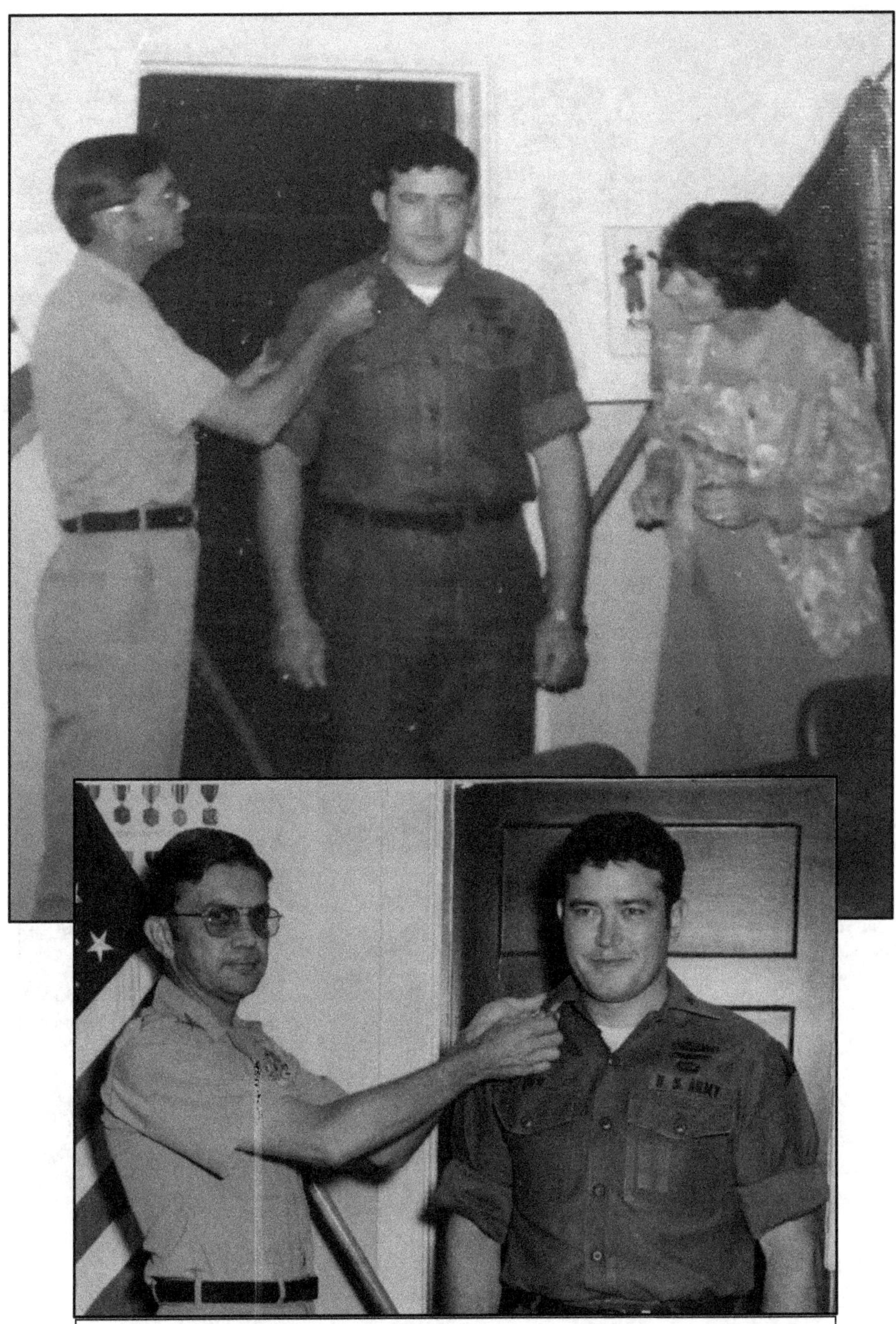

CPT HUN (WITH WIFE BRENDA) BEING PROMOTED TO MAJOR BY COL SUESS, PROVOST MARSHAL AT FORT HOOD

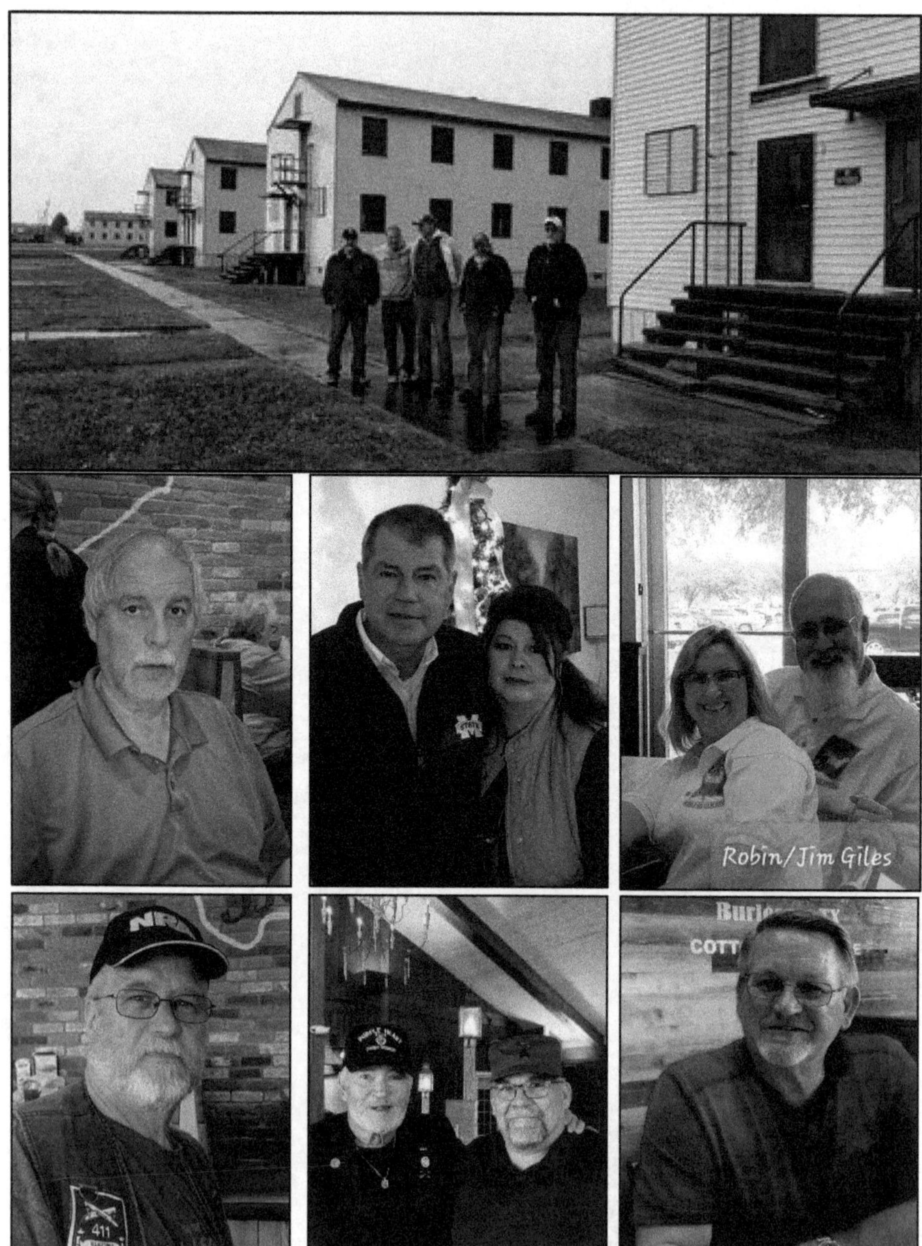

TOP ROW—OLD TIMERS RETURN TO FORT CHAFFEE
CENTER ROW—L-R: DAN MAPLES, MIKE & LESA JUDD, ROBIN & JIM GILES
BOTTOM ROW—L-R: JERRY MCKEAN, COL HUN & LANCE WARD, CR SINERUD

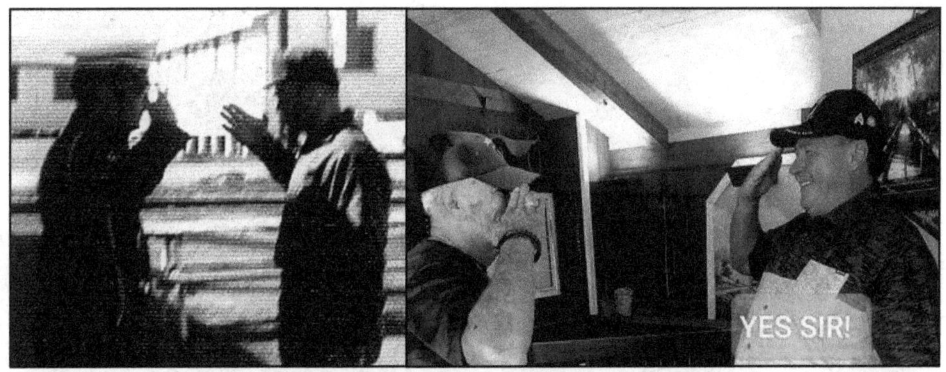

TOP ROW—SGT RON MORIN AND COL NICK HUN REINACTING SALUTE FROM FORTY-FIVE YEARS AGO
BELOW—L-R: —DEBBIE MORIN, MIKE JEWELL, COL HUN AT MIDDLEBURY, INDIANA—2019

TOP ROW—L-R: COL HUN, RON MORIN WITH HSM—MIDDLEBURY, IN
CENTER RIGHT—CR SINERUD, ED KLOBUCHIR, RON MORIN AT FORT HOOD, TX
BOTTOM—COL HUN, RON MORIN, MIKE JEWELL—MIDDLEBURY, IN

TOP ROW—SSG RUFFUS C. MILLER & WIFE FLOY LAVERN
BOTTOM—SSG MILLER & CR SINERUD

TOP ROW—L-R: JACKIE PRITCHARD, MIKE WOOD
BOTTOM—FORT CHAFFEE SWIMMING POOL (BEWARE OF THE SHARK!)

FT. HOOD SENTINEL. FT. HOOD. TEXAS

Three awards presented during monthly review

The 720th MP Bn. held it's monthly battalion review Thursday, Aug. 13. During the ceremony, the battalion commander, LTC George L. Nipper, presented three members of the 720th with awards for exceptional duty performance during Operation New Arrival, and two commanders with unit awards for support of Operation Task Force New Arrivals, Ft. Chaffee, Ark.

A highlight of the ceremony was the presentation of the Army Commendation Medal to SP4 Mark C. Allen of the 411th MP Co. and PFC Joel Allen of the 401st MP Co. Specialist Four Mark C. Allen received the award for highly commendable actions in saving the life of a Vietnamese child on July 10. Specialist Allen, while on MP roving patrol, was appcoached by a Vietnamese father who requested assistance in obtaining an ambulance so that his eight-month-old daughter might be transported to the hospital.

While awaiting the ambulance, the child stopped breathing. Allen immediately began artificial respiration which restored the child's breathing. Then after obtaining permission to leave his post, he transported the child to the hospital. Medical authorities credited his quick actions with saving the child's life.

Private First Class Joel Allen was awarded the Army Commendation Medal for similar circumstances on May 13. Allen was on duty at a guard post when he was approached by a Vietnamese father who asked that an ambulance be called for his young child, who was extremely ill in their family quarters. Allen notified another MP nearby to radio for an ambulance and then ran to the building and found the child with a high fever; her chest was hard and she was not breathing. He quickly started mouth to mouth resuscitation until the child started breathing again. Then along with the child's mother Private First Class Allen rushed the child to the hospital.

Both SP4 Allen and PFC Allen were cited for their quick, alert and compassionate actions which played a vital role in reviving the children. Their actions were a credit to themselves, their units, and the United States Army.

Specialist Five John A. Roth of the Headquarters Detachment received a Letter of Commendation for his outstanding performance of duty during Operation New Arrival. Roth maintained the entire S-1 section at Ft. Hood. His competance, diligence, devotion to duty and reliability greatly enhanced the operations of the battalion headquarters in the absence of the primary staff personnel.

The Commanders' Grand Job Certificate from the Commanding General of Task Force New Arrival, Ft. Chaffee, Ark., was presented to Headquarters Detachment of the 720th MP B., for exceptionally meritorious performance of it's mission in support of Task Force New Arrival. Brigadier General John Mackmull cited the unit for aggressively, meticulously and consistently accomplishing all assigned missions in a truly outstanding manner that proved invaluable to the smooth and efficient functioning of the operations at Ft. Chaffee.

The 411th MP Co. also received the Commander's Grand Job Certificate from BG Mackmull for outstanding performance of duties. The 411th MP Co. displayed initiative, resourcefulness and professionalism in the performance of their duties in both military and refugee areas of responsibility. The consistency with which they responded to routine and emergency situations alike was exemplary of the finest traditions of the Military Police, and was also instrumental in the smooth functioning of Ft. Chaffee during their time there.

Lieutenant Colonel Nipper then read the letters of appreciation from BG John Mackmull commander of Ft. Chaffee and also LTG Robert M. Shoemaker, commander of Ft. Hood, for the outstanding performance of the 720th personnel both at Ft. Chaffee and at Ft. Hood. Nipper added that he was pleased at the performance of exceptional duty under extremely difficult circumstances.

At the conclusion of the ceremony, families and visitors were treated to an excellent pass-in-review of the troops.

NOTICE OF AWARDS PRESENTATION TO 720TH MP BATTALION FOR OUTSTANDING PERFORMANCE AT FORT CHAFFEE—FROM THE FORT HOOD SENTINEL, FORT HOOD, TX

DEPARTMENT OF THE ARMY
411TH MILITARY POLICE COMPANY
FORT HOOD, TEXAS 76544

411th MP Company Platoon Break-down:

1ST PLATOON	2ND PLATOON	3RD PLATOON	HQ PLATOON
SSG MILLER	SFC JENNINGS	SFC THOMAS	1SG WALKER
SSG DANIELS	SSG HERRICK	SSG TYLER	SFC CULVER
SSG SKINNER	SGT RADER	SP6 MCFARLAND	SFC GROMMEL
SGT BECKLING	SGT BENNETT	SGT CARROLL	SSG MAGILL
SGT COULTER	SGT CARVER	SGT JACINTO	SSG DAVIS
SGT LEHMAN	SP4 HAMILTON	SGT ROBERTS	SSG WYLY
SP5 ESTRADA	SP4 MURPHY	SGT MAY	SP6 SEIDLER
SP4 KARL	SP4 BENNETT	SGT HAYES	SP5 FITE
SP4 ZANKER	SP4 CLAYTON	SP4 MOORE J.	SFC BARNES
SGT WATERS	SP4 JEWELL	SP4 WHITTAKER	SFC MOSES
SP4 MOLEMORE	SP4 KIERZEK	SP4 WALLACE	SP5 BACA
SP4 HENIGER	SP4 LANGLEY	SP4 BLALOCK	SP5 STANFORD
SSG DELGADO	SP4 NELSON	SP4 ANDERSON	SGT TEMPLE
SP4 BURNS	SP4 TAYLOR W.	SP4 CRAWFORD	SP4 BROOKE
SP4 GARDNER	SP4 WAGGONER	SP4 GREENUP	SP4 ALLEN
SP4 HOLMES	SP4 YANCHIK	SP4 HUNT	SP4 CHOUINARD
SP4 LEIGHTON	SP4 SHELDON	SP4 JACKSON	SP4 EDWARDS
SP4 MOSS	PFC GULLETT	SP4 MORIN	SP4 ELLIS
SP4 TAYLOR H.	PFC SHAFER	SP4 RILEY	SP4 MCKEE
SP4 VINCKERMAN	PFC TROTTER	SP4 ROBERTO	SP4 NANCE
PFC MANNING	PFC DAVIS	SGT ERWIN	SP4 SUGGS
PFC WRIGHT	PFC COWEN	PFC VAN DYKEN	SP4 VANDAALTA
PFC STRATTON	PFC HUBER	PFC SHAW	SSG BROWN
PFC ROBERTSON D.	PFC BELAFORD	PFC AUSTIN	SP4 HERNANDEZ
PFC AASGAARD	PFC TRAUTLOFF	PFC AYALA	PFC ANDERSON
PFC LACROIX	PVT HIRT	PFC LEMALLEN	PFC JOHNSON
PFC CAVAZOS	PVT MCGONGIE	PFC HUTCHISON	PFC PASCHAL
PVT DALLEZOTTE	PVT BRAGG	PFC SCHNEBERGER	SP4 SMITH D.
PFC GILES	PVT VERIBERS	PFC SHERMAN	SP4 STEPHENS
PVT HEANY	PVT PRITCHARD	PFC VAUGHAN	SP4 TATUM
PFC NORTHERN	PVT TAYLOR M.	PVT SMITH T.	PFC TREVAN
PVT POWELL	PVT MEYER R.	PVT KIRBY	PVT AMAYA
PVT ROBERTSON E.	SP4 BINDLEY	PVT MCMAHON	PFC GREEVER
PVT SHARPE		PVT MCCARTHY	PFC MACHUCA
PVT MARTELL			PVT PEREZ
PVT MEYER C.			PVT ERVING
PVT SQUIRES			PVT BROWN
PVT BOOK			PVT SUNDERLIN
PVT ALLEN M.			PVT DECASTRO
			PVT EASTHOM M.

FERNANDO DANIELS JR.
SSG
Opn/Tng NCOIC

OLD 411TH COMPANY ROSTER BY PLATOON
(COURTESY OF KATY FISHER-BINGHAM)

WEST POINT AND FORT MYER

What could you say about West Point? Certainly, it is a hallowed place for alumni, having produced some of our nation's greatest leaders who have brought us successfully through many wars going back to 1802, when the United States Military Academy was established. There are statues of Generals Douglas MacArthur and George Patton, among many others.

Trophy Point, overlooking the Hudson, presents a magnificent view that takes one's breath away. For both graduates and others, it is an honor to serve there. Working with the finest young men and women of our nation in the Corps of Cadets is to invest in the future of our great nation. Like in any organization, it is the quality of the people that produces excellence, and it is in the service to others that we find the pathway to the divine. Working at West Point epitomizes both potentialities.

As the installation deputy provost marshal, I had regular interface with much of the staff and faculty. Early on, while driving on post, I spotted MAJ Tom Johnson driving his car in front of me. Flashing my lights, I got him to pull over. As we both dismounted, he asked jokingly if I was going to give him a ticket. Tom and I first met while assigned to the 10th Special Forces in Germany, and then again in III Corps in Vietnam when I was the A Team XO at Dong Xoai. Tom fought with the mobile guerrillas under the leadership of

LTC Bo Gritz. It was good to see this brave officer, under such pleasant circumstances, alive and well. This was also my first association with First Lieutenants Mike Ryan and Steve Talt, two fine young officers from upstate New York. They have visited us numerous times during our journeys through life. Our families and theirs are close to this day.

COL Nipper decided to take a position with Bechtel Corporation and retired, being replaced by COL Bob MacDonald, another fine officer well respected in the Military Police Corps. In the interim, I had occasion to brief the West Point commander regarding an upcoming football game at Michie Stadium.

As I walked into the superintendent's office in my khaki uniform, MG Sidney B. Berry and about five of his staff were present. After I saluted, he graciously offered me a seat. I noticed the AK-47 we had given him, when he visited our A Team in Vietnam, mounted on a plaque behind his desk. When I mentioned that I liked his memento, he replied that it was given to him by some very special soldiers. With a big grin on my face I said, "Thank you, sir!"

Then he gave me a curious look. "You were at Dong Xoai?" he asked as he rose from his seat to shake my hand.

During our meeting, he asked if something could be done to clean up the sloppy-looking reserve MP's we brought in to provide additional traffic support on football Saturdays. I stated that I had not been there long enough to address that problem, to which he stated, that neither had he. After the laughter died down, I assured him that we would fix it.

Returning to my office, I asked our operations officer, CPT Chris Gershel, in to discuss the matter. Chris was a highly intelligent helicopter pilot who flew in Vietnam, and took up the challenge without delay.

The following Friday, prior to the next day's game, uniforms were inspected, boots were shined, and Chris gave free haircuts to all the supporting MPs who needed grooming. Many were cops from New York City who spread the word. As if by magic, the following week, and for the rest of the season, the reserve MP's came in clean and well-groomed. Chris was an excellent operations officer and a fairly good pilot, but a lousy barber. After a couple of years, he got out and became chief of police in Newburgh, NY.

On football Saturdays, I headed up a crew of military police in a room behind the superintendent's lodge from where we controlled security for the game, as well as traffic. It was interesting, as we could watch the game, while ensuring that entry of VIPs went smoothly and traffic flowed.

Army was having an excellent season in 1977 with eight wins, beating teams like Stanford. GEN Andrew Goodpaster, who had replaced MG Berry, was sitting in the lodge when our MPs had stopped the incoming flow of VIPs, as one of them did not have the required pass. As I went to investigate, there was then BG Michael J. Conrad with his wife. After rendering a hand salute, I crooked my right arm for Mrs. Conrad, which she took, asking General Conrad to come inside with me. I then informed General Goodpaster that General Conrad and his wife had arrived, to which he replied, "Please bring Mike in."

Army won the game, after which, General Conrad stopped by our command post and said, "Thanks Nick." Thus, my former commander from C Company, First Airborne Battle Group 187th Infantry, who gave me my first Article 15, would retire as a major general and continue to serve our nation as president of his West Point class, among other noteworthy undertakings.

COL Bob MacDonald was an excellent MP officer, for whom being provost marshal came naturally, and Chris Gershel was exceptional at running operations. CPT Joe Edwards, a USMA graduate, commanded the 57th MP Company in stellar fashion. Our MPs were specially selected and very high-quality soldiers not requiring much supervision. Because of this, my job as the deputy provost was relatively easy.

West Point provides exceptional facilities to assure the total development of the cadets. The gyms are well-appointed, there is a ski slope, and several football fields for practice. There are ponds to fish and deer to hunt for those so inclined. I enjoyed all the foregoing, along with much of the faculty and staff. It was fun to play flag football, and we won the post championship twice during our tour. Long Island University provided on-post classes, and I completed my studies for my master's degree in counseling. Our family was further blessed by the birth of our son, Nicholas Christopher Hun, on the 26th of May, 1977.

Among my duties was to coordinate with the AFL-CIO that represented the civilian employees on post. Colonel Mennona, the deputy chief of staff for personnel, and one of the finest officers I have had the honor to work with, was very astute. He may have picked me for this job as someone who could go low or high, depending on how negotiations were going. Needless to say, high standards were maintained in the civilian work force.

Over time, our relationship with the Union became quite amiable once everyone understood the other parties' position. During our three years at West Point, we had many visits from family and friends who also enjoyed the ambiance of this fine institution on The Hudson. Last year, Ambrose Brennan, my Special Forces A Team commander in Vietnam, and I returned to his alma mater on a football Saturday, and Army won! This assignment was personally and professionally rewarding and set the stage for our next assignment.

...

In January of 1980, I was selected to be the provost marshal at Fort Myer, Virginia, situated across the Potomac River from our nation's capital. Fort Myer, and nearby Fort McNair, in Washington, D.C. were considered showplaces, and much of the army's senior leadership lived there.

I was not sure that on-post housing would be available right away, which seemed to be the usual scenario every time we moved. Washington was so expensive that it really wouldn't have been worth the promotion without the advantage of living on post.

I drove from West Point to Fort Myer in the snow, leaving my family behind until I was sure I could get accommodations. I soon found out there were no quarters available for field grade officers, so my wife Brenda, daughter Tara, and my two-year-old son, Nicholas, stayed in Wheeling, West Virginia until May. Later, after some arm wrestling and politics and the help of COL George W. Kersey, the post commander, I was able to get a spacious, three-story house across from the officer's club.

COL Kersey proved to be a good friend and supporter of the military police during my tenure as provost marshal. He was a Citadel graduate and their first Fulbright Scholar. As our post commander, he accepted nothing but the best from all his charges. Highly intelligent and dedicated, it was a pleasure to work for him. Originally from Clarksburg, WV, he enjoyed socializing over "porch beer" at his quarters in the evenings as we planned the next day's activities.

Our military police had significant responsibilities regarding security at Fort Myer and Fort McNair. Though there were three entrances to the post, all staffed by our MPs, there was no particular security checks at the gates in early 1980. Consequently, the post was being used as a thoroughfare between Arlington, Virginia and Washington, D.C. by commuters. This brought in excess traffic and crime.

Having come from West Point where decals were required, I recommended a similar policy to COL Kersey who immediately liked the idea, as did then MG Robert Arter, the military district of Washington commander who hailed from Ohio. MG Arter was a great leader who had fought both in Korea and Vietnam as an infantry officer.

The word soon went out to the Pentagon, as well as the local newspapers, that access to Fort Myer would require a post decal or no entry. This brought a scramble for decals, particularly by the tens of thousands of civil servants who worked in the DC area. Many of these people liked to habituate the Fort Myer officer's club and could be found partaking of two-hour-plus lunches with libations before ending their "work days" in the early afternoon. We received numerous calls for low numbered blue decals, a status symbol of one's standing in the MDW community.

On the designated day, as the rules took effect, traffic outside the post was backed up for several miles, and many bureaucrats were late to work. On the brighter side, crime on post dropped dramatically, particularly after we required military identification prior to coming on post.

The next step was to conduct searches of vehicles for behavior involving alcohol or drugs. The final step involved searches of every fifth car entering the post.

It appears that our astute MPs did not always count correctly. An officer entering the post with his wife and children might not be stopped, though it was vehicle number five. On the other hand, a "beater" with a Deadhead sticker might be "designated" as number five, stopped, and searched. Regardless, our dedicated MPs netted big results, as evidenced by two large boxes of illicit drugs seized the first weekend. I showed these to a delighted COL Kersey before securing them in our evidence lockers at our MP station.

One evening, our MPs brought in a heavily built sergeant, quite drunk, who had been fighting in the NCO club. He was handcuffed very tightly and was uncomfortable when I saw him in the detention cell. As he had also fought our guys prior to his apprehension, I figured this was pay back. In any event, I informed him that we would remove the cuffs but any hostile action on his part might put him in the hospital. He believed me and no further hostilities took place as we removed the cuffs and sent him home.

We had regular guard mounts where our NCOs would inspect the oncoming shift. On one occasion, a young buck sergeant purposely burped in the face of one of our women MPs during an inspection. I informed CPT Waters, the very able commander of the 561st MP Company, that he could handle the matter any way he wanted, but that sergeant would not be working as an MP at Fort Myer anymore.

Given the sensitive mission, particularly VIP security on an installation where much of the army leadership resided, we did not allow for substandard performance or buffoonery. We established a Special Reaction Force that repelled in from helicopters when we opened our new provost marshal's office adjacent to the officer's club. During this well-attended event, I overheard COL Kersey tell one of the general officers watching, "The Hun comes in from the east and makes a big cut." With the strong support of LTG Arter, COL Kersey, and COL Russel, the MDW provost marshal, we had indeed established a reputation!

As two of the army's showplaces, Forts Meyer and McNair hosted numerous dignitaries, both foreign and domestic. Among them was a delegation from Hungary, headed by a Hungarian colonel who had little use for the Russian imposed communist dictatorship that still ruled the Eastern Bloc. As we were introduced, he had the widest grin when I spoke to him in Hungarian.

Things began to operate quite smoothly with the significant help of my deputy, CPT Dan Bullman. Dan had played football at Boston College and brought that demeanor with him to the job. While waiting for quarters, he graciously let me live in his place at Fort McNair while he was away training.

Once back, CPT Waters, Dan, and I would workout at the well-appointed gym at McNair. During one such period, CPT Waters said, "Why don't we box?" I said okay, as I had a little experience in pugilism as a kid and had more than my share of fights growing up as a refugee in Germany. However, no gloves were available, so he said, "Let's wrestle."

I could see the look in Dan's eyes, thinking this would not go well for his friend. At over six feet, Waters was quite impressive; however, I had wrestled in high school.

I quickly took him down, rolled him over, and pinned him when I heard an audible "crack." Unfortunately, his collarbone was broken, so we went to the hospital. He recovered but had to attend our weekly meetings with COL Kersey in a body cast for several weeks. After that, the challenges stopped.

Fort Myer was a great family post. COL Kersey's daughter, Jessika, would babysit our kids when she visited from New York. This gave my wife and I the opportunity to partake of much that DC had to offer, including dinner theaters and excellent restaurants in Georgetown.

I was soon integrated into the Regular Army, selected for lieutenant colonel, and received orders to attend Command and General Staff College at Fort Leavenworth, Kansas. Most importantly, our family was healthy and thriving.

FOOTBALL SATURDAY AT WEST POINT

INSET TOP LEFT—L-R: CPT AMBROSE BRENNAN, COMMANDER, AND 1LT NICK HUN, EXECUTIVE OFFICER, AT SPECIAL FORCES CAMP A-342 IN DONG XOAI, VIETNAM—1967
BOTTOM—RETURNING TO WEST POINT WITH MY A-TEAM COMMANDER IN VIETNAM. L-R: NICK HUN, AMBROSE BRENNAN

**57th MP COMPANY, WEST POINT, NY
1977 AND 1978 WINNING THE POST FLAG FOOTBALL
CHAMPIONSHIP. THAT'S ME #45.**

CGS COLLEGE AT FORT LEAVENWORTH

While attending the Command and General Staff College from 1981 to 1982, General Crosbie Saint pinned on my lieutenant colonel leaves while he jokingly chided me about needing a haircut. The good old days, when I still had hair, was often called, "The best year of one's army career," at CGSC. All of the officers selected were quite accomplished and, of course, the faculty and staff represented the upper tier of their various branches. There were foreign students from much of the globe, and it was interesting to see them interface on neutral soil. It was particularly poignant to see the Israelis and various officers from Muslim nations put their differences aside.

As a lieutenant colonel and assistant class leader, Brenda and I were invited to attend a lot of parties hosted by various allied officers. As soccer is a dominant world sport, our class had a formidable team with players from South America and Africa, among others. Given my European background, growing up with soccer, I made the team and even scored two goals in several games.

There was plenty of time to exercise, and I normally ran five miles, three times per week around the post. There were many more serious runners, particularly among the marine officers, who had run marathons in the past. Not to brag, but when we took our PT test, I took off my shirt and led from start to finish in the two-mile run, surprising the other ninety guys as well as myself. I guess they were pacing themselves a bit too long.

We lived in modest quarters on post surrounded by nice neighbors. There was no war, and except for the occasional tornado, there were few worries. After graduation, I and Ace Goerig, the class leader and army dentist, took a fishing trip to Alaska where we caught dozens of king salmon. My wife, Brenda, had her tennis; and our kids, Tara and Nicholas, had their friends. As the Frank Sinatra song goes, "it was a very good year."

CENTRAL AMERICA 1982-84

Having completed CGSC in the summer of 1982, our family of four was headed to Panama, where I was slated to be the southern command deputy provost marshal and provisional battalion commander for the Law Enforcement Activity (LEA). I sensed that this tour would be a bit different when we landed in Panama and several Hispanic individuals wearing *guayaberas* boarded the 747 and asked for LTC Hun. They were Military Police Investigators (MPI) and liaison with the Panama Defense Forces (PDF). They had been sent by COL Charles Madden to ensure his new deputy and family were expedited through customs.

We were dropped off at the Panama City Marriot, adjacent to the Pacific Ocean, for the night. While the setting was beautiful, Nicholas was extremely uncomfortable in this strange new country. While out at dinner that evening, I had left a tip for our waitress, including some quarters. Nicholas picked up some of the change with the intent to play video games. When I told him that money was for the waitress, our four-year-old lost it. He stood up, and with tears in his eyes, stated, "I don't like this country; I don't like these people; and I don't like you for bringing me here!" after which, he punched me in the nose. As I hugged him, I also teared up, realizing the cost that military families pay in serving our nation.

As our quarters at Fort Clayton would not be available for about a week, I called then MSG Sidney Jensen, who had been our senior commo man on our Special Forces A Team at Bunard in Vietnam. Sid was now in the 8th Special Forces working much of Central America from "safe houses." When I explained my dilemma, he asked if tomorrow would be soon enough to move on post? The next morning, our family was on Fort Clayton in one of the quarters designated for SF use.

Taking a lunch break from processing in, I bought a red bike at the PX and dropped it off at our temporary quarters. Returning home at the end of the day, Nicholas was happily riding his new bike with three little girls squealing as they chased him. Our benefactor, Sid Jensen, and I reconnected recently, and I plan to buy him a beer or three at the next SF reunion.

Serving in Central America during the eighties was both interesting and challenging as Castro was still spreading the mantel of communism in the region. Additionally, both Columbia and Panama were major exporters of illicit drugs to much of the world.

There was a well-attended welcoming party for the new deputy PM, including President Manuel Noriega, who was known affectingly to his detractors as "Pineapple Face." We were fortunate to have then BG Frederick F. Woerner, as the commanding general. Well versed in South and Central American culture and politics, he and his charming wife, Gennie, provided a pleasant work environment for the community while "keeping the wolf at bay."

The communist yoke had been imposed on Nicaragua and was threatening both Honduras and El Salvador, where armed insurgencies were in progress. The 193rd Infantry, and supporting units, ensured there would be no communist takeover of Central America.

Our military police, from both the 534th MP Company, commanded by CPT Jerry Prentice, and the 549th MP Company, commanded by CPT Dave Wardell, provided security for the Isthmus of Panama. Under the exceptional leadership of these fine officers, they were deployed on a regular basis, primarily to Honduras, as threats arose.

1SG Benito Colon Sanchez, from the 334th, was a tough Vietnam veteran that made sure the missions were accomplished, as well as caring for the welfare of our soldiers and their families. He and our operations sergeant, SFC Ron Herrington, a tough guy from Kentucky, worked together flawlessly. Given the foregoing, my job as the DPM was relatively easy and left time for leisure activities such as fishing, racquetball, and running.

Armed Forces Television recorded a lot of these activities in their programing and broadcast it across the Isthmus. I made several commercials about conditioning and securing property and became somewhat of a celebrity. Locals would point as I visited Panama City as if to say, "It's that guy!" COL Madden got a big kick out of this and would jokingly accuse me of cutting another commercial every time he went on TDY.

Our family took a vacation to the island of Contadora in November of 1983, and while watching the Dallas Cowboys on Thanksgiving, the commercial came up. There I was at the gym, pumping iron and stating, "I lift weights to stay in shape!" It was a bit too much even for me.

Each spring, there was a fifty-plus mile run across the Isthmus from the Atlantic to the Pacific Oceans. All the army units competed, along with the Panamanian National cross-country team. Our Law Enforcement Activity (LEA) had never done well, and COL Madden asked me to fix it.

We got our team together and trained for the event. I had not intended to participate but was faster than two young lieutenants, so I picked the third leg which was very hilly and no one wanted. Naturally, the Panamanian National Team won! Predictably, the 8th Special Forces guys came in second. Surprising all the 193rd Infantry guys, we came in third. Our military police shooters won the pistol competition as expected, but what was not expected was our winning both the rifle and the M60 competitions as well.

It was a good day for the MP Corps, and COL Madden was pleased. Under the exceptional leadership of General Woerner, morale was high in the brigade with a lot of competition between the units.

There were morning battalion runs where the various units would exchange pleasantries as they passed each other. The NCOs kept the troopers apart, and fisticuffs were kept to a minimum. That was not the case during riot control training, where the infantry served as belligerents and took their assignments too seriously.

I recall being in the front on one occasion, trying to disperse the crowd, when I was hit by caustic garbage that got in my eyes. CPT Prentice gave the order, and our MPs responded with more than sufficient force. Instead of dispersing, we took down the "rioters" and used plastic cuffs to hold them in the blazing sun. SFC Herington seemed to enjoy the melee while body slamming anyone foolish enough to get in the big man's lane.

During deployments, our military police provided security for projects expanding our footprint in the region. As airfields were built and other infrastructure established, I would fly in to see our soldiers.

On one such visit, I caught a courier flight that made a stop at Managua, Nicaragua, which was controlled by the communists under Daniel Ortega. Riding in the cockpit with the crew, I was well-armed with my M16 and three-hundred rounds of ammunition. As we were landing to drop off mail to the embassy, I noticed that anti-aircraft weapons on the side of the runway were tracking us. After landing and leaving my weapon in the cockpit, several of us stepped out of the ramp to stretch our legs. Approaching us were three uniformed men carrying AK-47 assault rifles. Two of them approached me and asked for my passport. I informed them that I was a US Army officer flying on a US Air Force plane and did not need a passport. One of them stated, "*Senor*, you must have a passport to come to our country."

I realized that the soldier was not Nicaraguan but Cuban and immediately informed him that this was not his country, and if I ever returned again, I certainly would not need a passport. Having served in the region, I understood the macho psyche of the culture.

As a last resort, I knew how the AK worked and considered "borrowing" it from him. In retrospect, I am glad it did not come to that. If it had, you probably would not be reading this right now.

The man and I looked into each other's eyes, and finally, his demeanor changed as he stated, *"No hay problema, Senor!"* with a smile. Problem solved!

The best MP Company designation that eluded us at Fort Hood with the 411th MP, was achieved by the 534th MP Company, under the command of CPT Gerald Prentice and 1SG Benito Colon. Army chief of staff, General John A. Wickham, presented the Jeremiah P. Holland award to our stellar MP in 1983 at a ceremony overlooking The Panama Canal at Fort Clayton.

The two years in Central America transitioned quite pleasantly for our family. We all thrived with Nicholas running track and Tara doing well in school, though I think the poverty she saw there impacted her, and does to this day. Brenda had her friends, and they played tennis several times per week while I was busy working both in and out of the country.

Among the dignitaries visiting the Isthmus was LTG Robert Arter, my former boss at Fort Myer, who had become the commanding general of the Sixth Army. At a welcoming reception in his honor, he approached General Woerner and I as we were chatting over a drink. As I stood next to these two great men, he put his arm around my shoulders. I was both surprised and honored by the subtle message that had been sent. I soon came down on the Lieutenant Colonel Command list, and our family departed for Fort Riley, Kansas where I would command the 3rd Battalion at the US Army Correctional Activity.

WITH FRIENDS IN PANAMA:
L-R: CAPTAINS GERALD PRENTICE, ROBERT PELEGREEN IN RED CAP.

TOP LEFT—MY WIFE BRENDA, SON NICK JR, AND DAUGHTER TARA IN PANAMA
TOP RIGHT—ME IN CENTRAL AMERICA—1983-84
BOTTOM—CENTRAL AMERICA IN THE 1980'S WHEN CASTRO WAS ATTEMPTING TO EXPAND HIS INFLUENCE

TOP—PANAMA CROSS COUNTRY RUNNERS
BOTTOM—L-R: TWO PDF (PANAMA DEFENSE FORCES OFFICERS), (CENTER) ONE OF OUR MPI (MILITARY POLICE INVESTIGATORS), ME IN FATIGUES, (FAR RIGHT) AIR FORCE POLICE

COL HUN AT CEREMONY WITH WIFE BRENDA, DAUGHER TARA, AND SON NICK JR

534TH MP CO—RIOT CONTROL TRAINING IN PANAMA
(COURTESY OF LTC JERRY PRENTICE-RETIRED)
LTC PRENTICE WAS AN "ALUMNUS" OF THE 401ST MP CO AT FORT HOOD, TEXAS, A SISTER COMPANY TO THE 411TH MP CO

MORE RIOT TRAINING IN PANAMA

TOP—OUR STRAF MILITARY POLICE UNDER THE PAINTING OF THE EAGLE AWARD THAT THE 534TH MP COMPANY RECEIVED

Page 8

534th MP Co wins Eagle, Holland Awards as the best in the Army

by Sp5 Susan Durban

There is a Fort Clayton based unit that has been successful in just about every task they've tackled in the past two years. Not only do they provide the daily details that raise and lower the flags, but they've fielded top quality sports teams, finishing third in football, second in softball and third in basketball.

They lead their battalion and the brigade in the best maintenance record and in funds generated by a unit of their size for local charities.

In the past year they accumulated many individual and unit Cutting Edge Awards, from the 193d Inf Bde commander, Brig. Gen. K.C. Leuer.

In 1980 the 534th Military Police Company (STRAF) was recognized as the best combat military police unit in Forces Command by winning the Eagle Award. They missed being named the best Military Police Company in the Army that year by a fraction of the total score.

For an encore in 1981 the 534th soldiers buckled down to the task and walked away with the FORSCOM Eagle Award and the Brig. Gen.Jeremiah P. Holland award for being the "Best" in the Army at their job.

How is it that the 534th MP Company (STRAF) excels in everything they do?

"Training was the key that gave us the edge for this year's award," said SSgt. Tom E. Lipford, 534th operations sergeant, "and it was probably 'the' most deciding factor."

"I think our participation in the many and varied support activities for the brigade and our own exercises gave us the expertise needed. One of the main reasons we're good at training is the amount of professionalism, at all levels, in the unit. From the commander to the lowest squad leader, everyone gives their best."

"It takes everyone's effort to succeed as we have. The commander set the example and our goal was to follow it," explained Lipford.

STRAF, Strategic Army Forces, personnel are not just ordinary, everyday policemen. These are the men that run POW camps, conduct convoy security, provide tactical operations security, man dismount points and perimeter defenses during any and all major field exercises.

These MPs work ten hour shifts. Before reporting for inspection, or pre-guard mount as they call it, they must get their weapons, ammunition and transportation, which includes a maintenance inspection.

Looking their best means a lot to these soldiers so they take pride in themselves and always look sharp for those daily inspections. Normally it takes a Military Policeman an houranda half to prepare for a full day's work.

"In all seriousness there is an air of togetherness and esprit de corps within the unit. It's displayed in everything the unit and its individuals do," Lipford said proudly.

CAPTAIN JERRY PRENTICE RECEIVING THE EAGLE AWARD FOR THE 534TH MP COMPANY

FORT RILEY & RECRUITING IN COLUMBUS

After a short leave in Wheeling, WV, our family, with one cat and a dog, drove to Fort Riley, Kansas and moved into our massive three-story quarters on Colonel's Row adjacent to a park. I reported into the US Army Correctional Facility at Camp Funston, under the command of COL Donald Greenwald.

The well-attended change of command ceremony included BG Henry Glenn Watson, who had been my battalion executive officer as a major at Dak To. Noticing the 173rd Airborne combat patch on my right shoulder, he asked me in which battalion I had served.

"Your battalion, sir!" I answered. Later, as we chatted, I thanked him for his leadership during those trying times.

It was not much later when the Fifth Army commander, LTG Edward A. Partain, came to Fort Riley. We had not seen each other since Vietnam in the 173rd Airborne. When he met Brenda at the reception that evening, he said, "Your husband is a brave man; those were tough times."

After serving in Central America in a STRAF unit at the cutting edge, working corrections stateside was much less exciting. Moreover, it was all new to me. While I was now well-versed in police work, corrections was a whole new game!

Our battalion was the largest correctional unit at Funston, responsible for over five-hundred incarcerated soldiers serving time for everything from AWOL to murder. Fortunately, we had an excellent staff with CSM Robert Dresden, MAJ Jack Hamell, MAJ Steve Presley, CPT Robert Pelegreen, and my executive officer, CPT Darla Elliot. COL Don Greenwald was a very cerebral, competent, and caring boss. His secretary, Pat Willey, was a mainstay of the activity, keeping all our units connected and informed.

. . .

The two-year command passed quickly, and I was now eligible for selection to the US Army War College, an essential step for promotion to higher levels. Then MG Ronald L. Watts, the 1st Infantry Division commander, served on the board that considered my case. When he returned, he told me how impressed he was with my military record. However, while I was selected, it was as an alternate. As my number did not come up, I was offered two options. I could teach at CGSC at Fort Leavenworth, or go to Columbus, Ohio and command a recruiting battalion. Often referred to as, "the toughest job in the army," it again was a brand-new game for which I had no training. As Brenda's parents were not well, I chose Ohio to be close to them. If I was going to make colonel, I would have to do it the hard way.

After completing the two-month Recruiting Battalion Commanders Course in the summer of 1986, we bought a three-bedroom house in Westerville, Ohio, a nice middle-class suburb twenty miles north of Columbus.

Tara, now thirteen, and Nicholas, ten, they enrolled in their fourth and third different schools, respectively. Westerville did have an excellent system where they both thrived. Tara studied drama, and Nicholas played soccer and football, while Brenda did substitute teaching to help make ends meet.

I was traveling several days a week through Central Ohio, and Parkersburg, West Virginia, inspecting our four companies and thirty individual recruiting stations. I soon discovered the competitive nature of this assignment as we worked to meet our monthly accession quotas. The numbers would magically be raised when they were met or exceeded for a few months. Basically, recruiting command would go where they could get them.

The army was looking for quality, which meant a high school diploma, no criminal record, and above the fifty percentiles on the ASVAB. Recruiting the cream of the crop of our young people was no easy task, given the generally upbeat economy at the time. Fortunately, we had mostly good recruiters, a fine staff, and four excellent company commanders in CPTs Lalonde, Lawyer, Debrueler, and Norton.

The driving force, father figure, and disciplinarian was the senior enlisted soldier in the battalion. We were blessed to have CSM Lamons, a sharecropper's son, who also fought with the 173rd ABN in Nam and brought the warrior spirit with him. While he was understanding and kind, he could be tough as nails if need be. Our recruiters got the message and performed well, making their "mission box" regularly and with integrity. This did not go unnoticed by our very astute boss, MG Allen K. Ono, who hailed from Hawaii.

As the commanding general, he regularly inspected the battalions and brought his great sense of humor with him. While riding together to the various companies, we would invariably pass a cemetery. His usual comment was, "Drive a little faster before they know we are here!" He was promoted to lieutenant general in 1987, becoming the first Japanese-American to achieve that rank.

One day, on the road, I took license to say to him, "It is not going to be easy in your next assignment!" When he gave me the inquisitive look of a general being counseled by a "light colonel," I followed with, "The Washington Bureaucracy has little chance of understanding your level of intellect or commitment."

As he smiled, I knew that we were back on the same page. Before departing for the Pentagon, as the deputy chief of personnel, he gave me an autographed photo, on which he wrote, "LTC Hun—you showed us that a tough, competent, and caring commander could build a winning team in Columbus. Thank you for your outstanding service."

High honor indeed from this great leader, statesman, and patriot who epitomized his words at the national level. The photo is prominently displayed in my, "I Love Me Room." Thank you, sir, and RIP!

DEPARTMENT OF THE ARMY
WASHINGTON, D. C. 20310-0300

June 14, 1988

Lieutenant Colonel Nicholas J. Hun
Commanding Officer
US Army Recruiting Battalion Columbus
200 North High Street
Room 114
Columbus, Ohio 43215-2483

Dear Nick,

Thanks for your letter of 9 June 1988.

Congratulations. I saw your name in January, but had to suffer in silence and explode with joy in private.

Have faith in our great Army. It is wiser and stronger than one thinks.

Sincerely,

AK Ono

Allen K. Ono
Lieutenant General, GS
Deputy Chief of Staff
for Personnel

CONGRATULATORY LETTER FROM LTG ALLEN K. ONO

OFF TO WEST VIRGINIA

Beating the odds during austere times, promotion-wise that is, I found my name on the army's list of newly selected colonels in January 1989. This was followed by numerous, kind congratulatory notes from colonels and general officers in whose commands I had served.

Once again, it was time for new digs and our family's final "Permanent Change of Station," (PCS). Discussions with the folks in Washington provided two offers. I could go to Tampa, Florida with an aviation assignment in the Army Reserve as their active-duty advisor, or to West Virginia as the senior army advisor to the National Guard. While my personal preference was to get back in the cockpit, Brenda's parents were still not well so we chose the latter option.

Following a short leave, we made the three-hour drive to Charleston, WV with our pooch, Snickers, and Dalton, our adventurous red cat. After two-plus hectic years in recruiting, I was ready for some solitude. My desire to get away was manifested by purchasing a beautiful three-story house with twenty acres on a mountaintop in Hurricane, WV.

There were many deer, bear, and foxes. Sadly, Dalton did not return from one of his nightly forays and may have been "outfoxed." The folks we purchased our house from had a lynx cat named Dudley that they left us. Dudley knew and ruled his territory, and like Dalton, he was fearless and kept the critters away from our house and curtilage.

One day, he tackled a large black snake on our front porch. Tara, being an animal lover, grabbed the cat and saved the snake, getting scratched up in the process. If you listened carefully in the evening, you could hear the faint sound of banjoes from the next hollow. Or should I say "holler?" We were now settled in "Wild and Wonderful" West Virginia.

While Tara's personality was well-suited for rural living, Nicholas not so much. They rode the school bus off the mountain to attend Hurricane Middle School, along with other kids from "the back forty." Not having local accents, they were often asked if they were from New York. They would both move on to Hurricane High School and continue being active. Brenda and I would watch Tara on stage in her drama club and Nicholas play football.

Working with the West Virginia National Guard was a pleasure! Competent and patriotic, they performed well under the strong leadership of their officers and senior NCOs.

Our Guard was greatly enhanced when MG Joseph J. Skaff became adjutant General in 1989. A distinguished soldier and statesman from West Point, the class of 1955, he had returned home to West Virginia where he would help lead the state to new heights of achievement across a broad spectrum.

I was honored to have him pin on my colonel's eagles soon after he arrived. MG Skaff brought many years of command experience with both active and reserve forces. His indominable spirit, coupled with an unrelenting quest for excellence, turned the West Virginia National Guard into a model for other states. Our success was verified through numerous field exercises, organizational readiness tests, and inspections. It culminated in the flawless deployment of five of our units to the first Gulf War in 1990.

The 201st Field Artillery Battalion from Fairmont was attached to the 18th Airborne Corps and made GEN Schwarzkopf's famous run to flank and destroyed the Iraqi Army after they had invaded Kuwait. Firing thousands of rounds of 155mm artillery, they were a major component in the success of Operation Desert Storm.

Significant air support came from the WV Air National Guard's 167th Tactical Airlift Groups flying their C-130 Hercules aircraft. The 4,200 soldiers and 2,100 airmen from West Virginia either deployed or supported this extraordinarily successful mission. They brought respect through victory to our state and nation as they helped obliterate Saddam's forces and free Kuwait.

The patriotic parades throughout the state for our returning warriors in early 1991 were reminiscent of the victory parades following World War II. As the West Virginia motto articulates—*Mountaineers Are Always Free!*

The relatively peaceful times following the first Gulf War provided opportunities for quality time spent with family and friends while off duty. Work involved significant travel, looking in on our units as they reconstituted and resumed their normal training.

I would hop on my Harley and ride east to Greenbrier County to visit the 150th Cavalry Regiment one week, then find myself up north in Wheeling hanging with the pilots of C Company of the 150th Aviation. Heading home the next day, I would stop in Fairmont to see the 201st and their APC mounted 155mm artillery that brought the max in Iraq. Not to say they needed much help from me, but I did enjoy the interface, particularly with the fine NCO's and troops.

Huntington was the home of the 2nd Battalion/19th Special Forces Group. Being a mere half-hour drive from our house, I would visit them and jump stories would abound. One day, group commander COL Allen Tacket asked if I would consider jumping with them, and of course I said "Yes!" When I put in for permissive jump status, General Skaff was kind enough to recommend approval to First Army, where it was promptly turned down. Ironically, the same thing happened when I volunteered to go fight in the Gulf War back in 1990. I guess you can only have so much fun in one army career. Al Tacket was later promoted and commanded the Guard, while the 2/19th sent its Green Berets to fight in Afghanistan where they distinguished themselves fighting on horseback, among other adventures.

Governor Caperton appointed General Skaff as the secretary of military affairs and public safety for the state. His responsibilities included oversight of the army and Air Guard, as well as prisons, jails, and the state police, among others. A heavy load indeed for even the strongest commander like General Skaff. The issue was further exacerbated by our antiquated prison system, which was in perpetual chaos.

As I completed thirty years of army service, three inmates serving life sentences for murder escaped from the state's antiquated maximum custody facility in Moundsville, prompting a search for a new prisons' chief. Having military corrections experience and General Skaff's recommendation, Governor Caperton appointed me the commissioner of corrections in March of 1992.

At my retirement ceremony, I was presented a plaque with the names of twenty-one command sergeants major, thanking me for my service. As General Skaff pinned on my legion of merit, I left the roles of the United States Army. I am still warmed by my association with the fine men and women of the West Virginia National Guard.

TOP—(LEFT) BIG JACK YEAGER, (CENTER) MG JOSEPH SKAFF, (CENTER REAR) COL HUN—DURING AN FTX IN 1990
BOTTOM—TRAINING WITH M-60 MACHINE GUN AS SENIOR ARMY ADVISOR TO WEST VIRGINIA NATIONAL GUARD—1990

MY RETIREMENT CEREMONY FROM THE UNITED STATES ARMY WITH MG JOSEPH J. SKAFF AND THE SERGEANTS MAJOR OF THE WEST VIRGINIA NATIONAL GUARD IN 1992

ON TO CIVILIAN LIFE

Upon retirement, I took advantage of the opportunity to move our family off the mountain to the city of Hurricane at government expense. We built a two-story brick house, sandwiched between the high school and the city park, where we still reside. From there, I made the daily commute to my office in my government sedan, adjacent to the golden-domed capitol building in Charleston.

There was little time spent there, except for hearings when the legislature was in session. The action was mostly in the field, inspecting the dozen facilities holding inmates throughout the state. Of particular concern were our maximum and medium custody facilities in Moundsville and Huttonsville.

My initial visit to the Old Pen, built in 1863, revealed something resembling the painting, *Dante's Inferno*. Entering, I noticed the old gray walls with their gun towers looming eerily over the landscape. My first stop was at the infamous North Hall, holding sixty of the most vicious inmates in five-by-seven cells, resembling a slightly enhanced version of cages used for greyhounds at the state's dog tracks. Inside, I found our extremely harried correctional officers, on twelve-hour shifts, subduing several violent inmates. It was 11:00 a.m., and the morning bacon was piled high on trays while three of the culprits were handcuffed naked to poles. The hall was flooded by water hoses used to quell the riot, and two guards stood with shotguns at the ready behind a food stained, plexiglass wall.

Apparently, the breakfast meal did not suit the sensitive pallets of the North Hall inmates. Having access to newspapers, the caged ones figured out who I was. Among the milder things they hollered at me was, "We know where you live; our friends will kill you and your whole family." Alrighty then! My son and his friends still joke about my having a gun in every room.

Huttonsville was not much better. Although we had a very competent warden in Bill Duncil, and a stellar deputy in Steve Yardley, the facility was overcrowded and understaffed. Moreover, with Moundsville at overflow, numerous high-risk inmates populated this facility. The inadequate staffing resulted in having no correctional officers in the dorms on the night shift. Instead, cages had been built on each of the eight floors where the correctional officers were locked in like they were the inmates.

On the dorms, there was the usual mayhem, along with forced sodomies on younger inmates. It did not take an advanced degree to determine that things were way out of kilter. The issue was somewhat abated one evening when there was a mini riot on the dorm.

One of our stellar women sergeants went in with a small team and restored order. The following day, I drove to Huttonsville, promoted her to lieutenant, and awarded her a hundred-dollar bond for exemplary duty performance.

Soon after, with the help of Governor Caperton and the WV Legislature, additional funds were allocated to Huttonsville, allowing us to staff the dorms around the clock. Simultaneously, we instituted a policy to beam up any troublemaker to the place no one wanted to go—the West Penitentiary! Life expectancy could be short there.

Of course, none of the foregoing was acceptable to Governor Caperton, General Skaff, or myself. The Old Pen with its gallows and "Old Sparky," the electric chair, were destined to be relegated to the annals of history, along with the eighty-plus inmates who were murdered or died by their own hands. This does not include the over one-hundred souls who swung on the gallows or the nine who left via "Old Sparky."

George Trent, the director of the DOC's training academy in West Liberty, was appointed warden of the Old Pen. With the able assistance of Paul Kirby, his deputy, and Tony Lemasters, his chief of security, things rapidly changed. Soon, the crazies no longer ran the asylum.

We were blessed to be reinforced by our stellar state police, the fourth oldest state police agency in the US. During one of our early meetings with their rapid reaction force, I told them that I was not necessarily looking for blood to be shed. However, if the prisoners started to riot, it should end quickly and decisively. The time for games was over!

The message was well received by the fine men and women of our state police. Under the exceptional leadership of Colonel Thom Kirk, the state police superintendent, they would very quickly respond to any problem in our correctional facilities. This was exemplified during an incident in early '93 as a fight on the yard began. This was an often-used ruse to distract the officers while more heinous activities were in the offing.

Tony Lemasters, knowing the state police had his back, went on the yard and confronted the actors with some reality therapy. They needed to stop now or suffer the consequences. Tony is a tough guy, and they became quite compliant.

While a new maximum custody facility was being built in Fayette County, Governor Caperton and General Skaff convinced the legislature to double the pay of our correctional officers from a measly $1,200 per month to $ 2,400. Staff morale was quickly enhanced and performance was significantly improved. Moreover, the often-used tactic of calling off sick to allow another correctional officer to draw overtime pay was considerably reduced.

The Old Pen in Moundsville was closed in early 1995 with the remaining six-hundred inmates transferred to the newly built, state of the art prison in Mount Olive. Colonel Kirks' troopers escorted the cuffed, orange-clad prisoners in buses without incident. At Mount Olive, the now rejuvenated correctional workforce was waiting to process them into their new home.

With the help of federal grants, numerous new programs were brought online to facilitate the transition of felons to contributing members of society. Most significantly, PSIMED, a West Virginia mental health company under the leadership of their CEO, Mr. Terrence Rusin, brought first-rate services to our prisons and jails. With his own version of "Charlie's Angels," namely, Rita Pauley in operations, Trudy Blaylock in programs, Freddie Sizemore in administration, and Kelly Sowards, his trusted assistant, they comprised a formidable team. Working closely with our very able deputy commissioner, Manfred Holland, they helped bring our prison system from the dark ages into the twenty-first century.

None of this could have transpired without a buy-in by the judiciary. Exceptional support came from Judge Todd Kaufman, who brought the wisdom of Solomon to the bench. His benevolent altruism greatly enhanced West Virginia's rehabilitative programs. As the administration changed, I left state government in 1997.

Sadly, the next two commissioners left us to their final reward rather quickly. Jim Rubenstein then took the helm as commissioner in 2001. From a family of renown public servants, he was well-versed with twenty-plus years in the field. He served with distinction for an additional sixteen years in this highly demanding position. Under his strong leadership, our prison system received the coveted American Correctional Association (ACA) accreditation.

Out on my own after thirty-seven years of military and state government service, I went into private business. After getting my private investigator license, I sublet office space from local attorney, William "Chip" Watkins, three miles from our home and opened AVAR Investigative Services.

Being a PI was interesting work. One sees all manner of cases, from cheating spouses to vehicle accidents, along with graft and larceny in the business world. At fifty dollars an hour, I was well compensated, and my phone rang regularly.

One of the ladies at the DMV, where I checked on the ownership of vehicles that were found parked at various hotels, commented to her co-workers, "Nick is really a good PI because he knows what to look for." Not exactly sure what she meant, but I told her that I appreciated the recognition, chuckles all around!

As I set my own schedule, I could delve out into various other enterprises. Among these were consulting work for several national companies. I also did some work for our state attorney general.

While visiting Charleston one day, I dropped in to see LTC Herb Latimore, who had replaced me as the senior army advisor to the National Guard. His prior assignment had been at Fort Leavenworth, Kansas as a strategic planner, working with Northrop Grumman, conducting warfighter exercises. He asked if I had any interest in such? I did miss the military, and with his recommendation, I was hired by the NG as a part-timer, planning exercises as well as actual wartime deployments for the next twelve years. I enjoyed the travel, the camaraderie, and being relevant on the world stage in my sixties.

Sometimes, my itinerary would allow me to adjust my flight home and spend a week in exotic places. Chief among these was Budapest and Bucharest, where I spoke the language, and the sunny beaches of Costanza, Romania.

My work, essentially, involved studying and analyzing global events relating to matters military. As it happened, the second Iraq war was in the offing in 2003. Then army chief of staff, GEN Shinseki, came to Fort Leavenworth for an update and our findings. I happened to be the briefer and explained that the Iraqi Army had many vulnerabilities and could be defeated as they had been in the first Gulf War. However, the country was very unstable; and the Shia and Sunni would turn on each other, and a civil war would likely ensue. Any occupying force would be caught in the middle. Moreover, any invasion would further embolden our real enemy, Iran, with their mischief.

General Shinseki took the word back to the second Bush administration, where it was not well received, and General Shinseki retired. The ensuing Gulf War lasted until 2011 costing thousands of US lives, while up to a million Iraqis may have perished.

While traveling by train in Hungary, some young people sat in our enclosed coach. When the Iraq issue came up in our discussions, one of them said, "It's all for oil!" I had no retort.

TOP LEFT—ADDRESSING THE CORRECTIONAL STAFF AS COMMISSIONER OF CORRECTIONS AT MOUNT OLIVE MAXIMUM CUTODY FACILITY IN WV—1994
TOP RIGHT—PLAQUE ON NEWLY OPENED REGIONAL JAIL IN CHARLESTON, WV
BOTTOM—COMMISSIONER OF CORRECTIONS FOR WV—1992

TOP—WITH OUR DIVISION OF CORRECTIONS COLOR GUARD—1994
BOTTOM—L-R: WITH WARDEN WILLIAM DUNCIL AND MG SKAFF—1995

TOP—COMMISSIONER HUN CHILLING IN CHARLESTON
BOTTOM—REGIONAL JAIL OPENING CEREMONY WITH GOVERNOR CAPERTON, MG SKAFF AND MEMBERS OF THE REGIONAL JAIL AUTHORITY

WORKING FOR THE VETERANS ADMINISTRATION

Working as a PI and part-time with Northrup Grumman left ample time for leisure activities. Racquetball was in the offing year-round, and I would hit the links during spring and summer with monotonous regularity.

One spring day in 2001, I ran into Mr. Jesse Coulter on a local course in Institute, WV. Jesse had marine corps service and was the team leader at the Charleston, WV Veterans Center. As we chatted about our life experiences, he mentioned that he had an opening for a counselor and would I be interested. I applied and got the job. Within a few months, the team leader's position opened in Huntington, WV, and I was selected by our headquarters in Baltimore to fill that slot.

Reporting in for duty, I found a very able group of counselors, particularly Ms. Bobby Michael, who had a son serving in the Gulf. We provided individual as well as group counseling services for combat veterans from World War II to the ongoing conflicts in the Middle East. Bobby had a large group of Vietnam guys who made great progress under her benevolent guidance. I would cover her group when she was on leave with relative success as they saw me as one of them.

One of our heroic veterans was John Goodwin, a marine who saw much combat in Vietnam. In one of our group sessions, I inadvertently teared up, something the counselor is not supposed to do. His astute comment was, "He has it worse than we do." John gave me several poems he had written that appear at the end of this book. May he RIP!

While most of our clients were legit, the occasional "stolen valor" phony would show up. As I filled in for one of our less experienced counselors, a veteran showed up wearing a government issued field jacket with a 101st Airborne patch on his left shoulder and a Special Forces patch on his right. I greeted him with the often-used term among SF guys, "Hey, snake eater!" As he seemed to not understand, I asked in which SF unit he had served. His reply was that he could not discuss it because it was "black ops" and, technically, they did not exist. Having more than passing knowledge of this type of warfare, I sensed that he was not of that ilk.

Checking his file, I noted that he was drawing 100% disability for PTSD. His DD Form-214 revealed information that had been erased and typed over. In the portion designating specific areas of service, I found the comment, "In the bush."

Alrighty then. While I understand the upside of such endeavors, I really do not view them as compensatable by the VA. I promptly reported the fabrication to the regional office. After their initial reluctance to accept that an error had occurred, the ensuing investigation revealed that, in fact, the claimant's military service did not exist.

As our vet center was located on Fourth Avenue in Huntington in an area used by drug addicts to shoot up and prostitutes to ply their trade, I lobbied Baltimore for a new venue. My request was approved by our tough and very able director, Mr. Phil Hame.

Shortly, we moved to a brand-new building, conveniently located by Interstate 70, from where we could serve veterans from Ohio, Kentucky, as well as West Virginia. Remembering our incarcerated veterans from my days as commissioner of corrections, I began an outreach to our maximum custody facility at Mount Olive. Twice a month, I would make the two-hour drive for group counseling sessions with the incarcerated veterans. Receiving exceptional help from Mr. Stephen Hatfield, a veteran of the 82nd Airborne who was doing time for a crime of passion, we had a very cohesive group that served as a model of good behavior for the institution.

Thanks to our fine staff, we made exceptional progress in our center, which was noticed by our new VA director, General Shinseki. During one of his visits, we reminisced about our earlier meeting at Fort Leavenworth and the second Iraqi War. I thanked him for speaking truth to power, to which he responded, "I did it for the troops!"

After two productive years in this position, I received an offer for promotion with a move to the VA Regional Headquarters in Baltimore. Being quite content in West Virginia, I declined and went back to working for Northrop Grumman, PI work, and consulting. I turned the Mount Olive group over to Bobby Michael, where she was well received and proved most effective. Jack Husted, a Vietnam vet and marine, became the team leader. The center was in good hands.

LIVING THE DREAM

As work allowed, I have traveled back to my roots in Hungary from where I left as a kid with only the clothes I wore on my back. Now, seeing Europe as an American citizen who helped keep the continent free, it is a special thrill.

While visiting the Czech Republic several years ago, Brenda was tired after a long day of touring. I decided to go out for a beer. The closest bar had a figure of a scantily dressed young lady under a sign that stated—*Dancing Girls 24/7*. Stepping inside, I found the bar packed. There was only one chair available among a group of British men in their thirties who were there for a soccer tournament. They asked me to join them. As I did, a burly guy across from me, who was very drunk, asked if I was a Czech. I told him I was an American, to which he responded, "Love you mate, mind if I have a drink of your beer?" He then chugged my beer and said, "I will knock your f—king head off!"

Not wishing to lose my head sitting down, I stood up and assumed a fighter's stance. As the place fell silent, he said, "You are a bad MF!" Then he went to the bar where he intentionally bumped each sitting patron, none of whom wanted to take him on. As his buddies got up to take him out, they glanced at me and said, "Too drunk!"

Since my beer was gone, I started to walk out when an attractive waitress brought me a jumbo Budweiser that I had not ordered. The four remaining guys in the group had bought my beer and again asked me to join them.

After much discussion, we discovered we had some things in common. They were conservative coal miners from Great Britain who said they didn't appreciate their country being swarmed by Muslims "ten to a flat." Having traveled in Europe, seeing much of the same, it was hard to disagree. When asked where I was from in the States, I said, "West Virginia." Then they all sang the John Denver song, "Country Roads," with much feeling.

Around 3:00 a.m., after too much beer, I informed them I was an old man and should get back to the wife. They opined that it had not been an "old man" who was well-prepared to kick their buddy's ass! We left as friends, and I wandered back to the hotel quite sedated.

I have also had the privilege of returning to Vietnam where I have never been treated better. From Hanoi to the Delta, the people have great respect for America. Despite their socialist government, they want to be more like us. Certainly poignant, considering more than a million Vietnamese died during the "American War."

The beacon of freedom shines brightly for even the most oppressed. In my advanced seventies, I look back on my military career, my subsequent work with the prison system, and the Veterans Administration with fond memories. I feel good about the path God has chosen for me and hope to continue to contribute to society. I strongly believe that it is in the service to others that we find the pathway to the divine. Not to imply that I am ready for the hereafter! Not yet, as there is still much to see and do. Adventures abound and there are wonderful places to visit.

Then there is the current state of our Great Nation! With our National elections now over, I will continue to speak my truth to all who will listen. We must save our great republic from those who would destroy it. Anarchists get no sympathy from me! Neither does the poison of liberalism, which then morphs into socialism, and finally communism—the ultimate vexation to the human spirit.

I will be promoting the principles of freedom that our country has stood for since its founding. I strongly believe in our constitutional government with equality and opportunity for all our citizens. I am supporting a strong and viable military. I believe in the right to keep and bear arms and the freedom to worship. I want for my adult children and young grandchildren to be able to choose their own pathways, including how and where they are educated. As I look forward to the next election, I plan to vote to retain the electoral college, so a few heavily populated liberal bastions do not control the future of America.

I am voting for a supreme court that interprets our constitution and does not rewrite it. I am voting against open borders while welcoming legal immigrants. I strongly support racial equality without special privilege for any race or class. I am supporting our brave police who keep us safe, and a judicial system that keeps violent criminals off our streets and in prison where they belong.

Having seen the ravages brought by Marxist governments up close and personal, I will never capitulate to them. Having shed my blood in the defense of liberty as a soldier, I now look forward to the continued blessings of liberty. God Bless the United States of America.

THE END

HANGING WITH PRESIDENT REAGAN AT FREEDOM SQUARE IN BUDAPEST

TOP—THANKSGIVING 2019
BOTTOM LEFT—R-L: MYSELF WITH WIFE BRENDA, AND NIECE LYNDSEY AT HUNTINGTON, WV 7-27-2019
ABOVE RIGHT—ME & NIECE KRISTINA

TOP—RETURN TO VIETNAM—VISIT TO A FLOATING MARKET IN SAIGON

BOTTOM LEFT— ENJOYING RIVER CRUISE IN LAKE BALATON IN HUNGARY WHILE ON BREAK FROM WAR FIGHTER EXERCISES—2007

FRONT ROW—L-R: GABRIEL DORRIS, BRENDA HUN, CASANDRA DORRIS, ELLA HUN, NICK HUN

BACK ROW STANDING—L-R: TARA HUN DORRIS, DYLAN DORRIS, OWEN HUN, DR. NICHOLAS C. HUN

CHRISTMAS AT THE GOVERNOR'S MANSION

TERMS AND DEFINITIONS

A

A-CAMP—In Vietnam, a Special Forces detachment tasked with training and advising South Vietnamese and CIDG forces conducting combat operations in forward areas. Also known as an ODA (Operational Detachment Alpha). SF personnel assigned here are known as an A-Team.

AH-1 COBRA GUNSHIP— (See SLICKS AND GUNS)

AO—AREA OF OPERATIONS

ÁO DÀI—A traditional gown-like dress worn by Vietnamese girls and women. There are several pronunciations for the word, but the most common is probably "ow-zai."

ARVN—ARMY OF THE REPUBLIC OF VIETNAM (South Vietnamese Army)

ARTICLE 15—Non-judicial punishment meted out to soldiers for minor infractions, usually handled by the soldier's immediate commander.

A-TEAM—See A-Camp.

AIDE-DE-CAMP—Assistant to a high-ranking military officer.

B

BAC SĨ—Vietnamese word for "doctor." Also used for the SF Medic.

BANDOLIER—A belt of ammunition fed into a machine gun.

BOQ—BACHELOR OFFICER'S QUARTERS

BAZOOKA—See M20A1

B-TEAM—A Special Forces headquarters AOB (Advanced Operational Base) providing command and support for A-Camps.

BIG RED ONE—FIRST INFANTRY DIVISION

BRACKET—A technique used by grenadiers to site in a target by placing "test" shots beyond and before the desired target.

BUNARD—Special Forces A-Camp A-344 located in the far northern edge of War Zone D in Vietnam.

C

C-47—Fixed-wing, WWII propeller airplane (civilian designation DC-3). Used as a platform for a weapons system known as "Puff the Magic Dragon," or "Spooky." See Puff the Magic Dragon.

CBU—CLUSTER BOMB UNIT—A free-falling bomb dropped from an aircraft that ejects individual exploding "bomblets." Effective against enemy personnel and soft-skinned targets.

CIB—COMBAT INFANTRY BADGE—A United States Army military decoration awarded to infantrymen and Special Forces soldiers from the rank of colonel and below, who fought in active ground combat while assigned as members of either an Infantry or Special Forces unit of brigade size or smaller. (Wikipedia)

THE COWBOYS—335th ASSAULT HELICOPTER COMPANY—The Cowboys directly supported the 173rd Airborne Brigade in combat for over 30 months in Vietnam.

C-RATIONS—A generic term for a prepackaged combat meal issued to individual soldiers when fresh hot food is not available.

CENTRAL HIGHLANDS OF VIETNAM—A mountainous plateau region in Central Vietnam near the Cambodian and Laotian borders.

CHARLIE—Slang term used by US Military personnel for the Viet Cong. Other names were Charlie Cong, Charles, Chuck, and Victor Charlie, et al.

CHERRY RUN—Any "first time" experience for a soldier.

CHERRY WINGS—Slang term for the parachutist badge awarded to a soldier who has completed the Basic Airborne Course.

CHICKEN PLATE—Slang for an armor-plated vest worn by pilots and crew for protection.

CIDG—CIVILIAN IRREGULAR DEFENSE GROUP—Indigenous people such as the Montagnards and Cambodians that were recruited, trained, and advised by the Special Forces to fight the enemy.

CHI LINH—Special Forces A-Camp (A-333), 16km (10 miles) west of Dong Xoai in Vietnam.

COLLECTIVE—Left side hand control on a helicopter. Makes the helicopter go up and down by changing the pitch of the blades. It also houses the throttle (motorcycle style "twist"). See Pedals.

COMMO MAN—A soldier whose specialization is that of Radio Operator. Same as RTO.

CONEX—Steel storage container used by the military.

CONGRESSIONAL MEDAL OF HONOR or CMH—The United States highest military decoration for acts of valor.

CORDITE—A smokeless propellant or gunpowder.

C-TEAM—The Special Forces headquarters in command over A and B detachments.

CYCLIC—Right side hand control on a helicopter (like a "joystick"). Controls the helicopter's direction of movement (forward, backward, sideways). See Pedals.

D

DEUCE AND A HALF—Two-and-a-half-ton, 6X6, military truck

DISTINGUISHED SERVICE CROSS—The second highest US Military award for extraordinary heroism below that of the CMH.

DMZ—DEMILITARIZED ZONE—Usually a geographic border marking a division between two different armies, e.g., the border between North and South Korea.

DONG XOAI—Special Forces A-Camp A-342 located approximately 88km (55 miles) north of Saigon. Abbreviated "DX."

E

ELEPHANT GRASS—A tall, sharp-edged tropical grass in Vietnam that provided good cover for enemy troops.

F

FAC—FORWARD AIR CONTROLLER—See L-19/O-1 CESSNA BIRD DOG

FIDDLER'S GREEN—A fanciful place in the afterlife where soldiers and sailors go after death.

FIELD GRADE—Commissioned US Army officers, grades O-4 thru O-6 (Major, Lieutenant Colonel and Colonel).

FLAK—Used as a general term in the military for flying shrapnel from exploding ordnance in a battle. Also, FLAK VEST. A ballistic vest or jacket worn to protect a soldier against flak.

FNG—F**KING NEW GUY—A derogatory term for a new, untested soldier in Vietnam; a greenhorn or newbie.

FLETCHETTE ROUND—Anti-personnel artillery round that fires nail-like projectiles made of steel.

FRAG—A slang term for "fragmentation grenade." Also, the act of killing or attempting to kill one's superior officer or NCO with a grenade to make it look like they were killed in combat. The term was coined during the Vietnam War.

FRATRICIDE—In war, being killed by your own fellow troops—same as "friendly fire."

FREE-FIRE ZONE—An area of open combat and unrestricted fire.

FREE GUNS or FREE 60—Door gunners on Huey helicopters would sometimes suspend their M60 machine guns from bungee cords to give them more maneuverability, or just deploy them by hand.

F**K YOU LIZARD—A slang term given by US soldiers to the Tokay Gecko lizard of Southeast Asia because its mating call resembles the expletive "F**k you!"

G

GCI—GAS CHROMATOGRAPH INTOXIMETER—Similar to a Breathalyzer. An instrument that measures blood-alcohol content.

GP MEDIUM—GENERAL PURPOSE TENT

GUAYABERAS—A Cuban, men's summer shirt, worn outside the trousers, distinguished by two vertical rows of closely sewn pleats running the length of the front and back of the shirt. (Wikipedia)

H

THE HERD—The 173RD AIRBORNE BRIGADE

HE—HIGH EXPLOSIVE

HT-10—Handheld radio used in Vietnam.

HIGH ANGLE OF FIRE—Artillery fire delivered at angles of elevation greater than the intended maximum range of the gun and ammunition resulting in diminished accuracy.

HILL 875—An operation to take Hill 875 during the Battle of Dak To in November of 1967, resulting in heavy US losses, particularly to the 173rd Airborne Brigade.

HOG PODS—Rocket pods (launchers) mounted to the sides of a helicopter.

HOT LZ—An LZ (Landing Zone) where troops and aircraft are receiving enemy fire. To "come in hot," means to fly in on an assault with guns blazing. See LZ.

I

IFR—INSTRUMENT FLIGHT RULES—Flying by instrumentation.

J

JUMP WINGS—Parachutist Badge awarded to all military personnel who have completed the US Army Basic Airborne Course at Fort Benning, Georgia. (Wikipedia)

JUNGLE ROT—A chronic ulceration of the skin thought to be caused by a polymicrobial infection, common in tropical climate. (Wikipedia)

K

KIA—KILLED IN ACTION

L

LEG or STRAIGHT LEG—A derisive term for a soldier who is not Airborne qualified.

LISTENING POST—Guard duty where a soldier, or several soldiers, would set up well beyond the safety of the perimeter to detect enemy activity and forewarn the camp.

LZ—LANDING ZONE—A place cleared out in the jungle for helicopters to land. See HOT LZ.

L-19/O-1 CESSNA BIRD DOG—A small, fixed-wing, single prop, light observation plane used primarily for reconnaissance by an FAC (Forward Air Controller). The FAC would fly above the battlefield in communication with the troops below. As a spotter, he identified enemy positions and relayed the information to attack aircraft and artillery units. FACs were able to mark targets with WP (white phosphorus) rockets and also advise of needed corrections and adjustments by direct observation.

LLDB—LUC LUONG DAC BIET *same as VNSF*—VIETNAMESE SPECIAL FORCES

M

☙ MACHINE GUNS, RIFLES AND HANDGUNS

AK47—Soviet automatic Kalashnikov rifle 7.62 x 39mm. See SKS Rifle.

BAR—M1918 BROWNING AUTOMATIC RIFLE—US Caliber .30-06 Springfield. A fully automatic rifle used primarily during WWII and Korea. The BAR was essentially replaced by the M60 machine gun.

M1/ M2 CARBINE—US .30 CAL. CARBINE—A carbine developed during WWII for use by support troops where the M1 Garand proved too heavy and cumbersome. Also used by indigenous forces in South Vietnam.

M1 GARAND RIFLE—US .30-06 CAL. standard US rifle of WWII and Korea.

M14 Rifle—US 7.62MM RIFLE—Same caliber as .308 Winchester. Standard rifle of the US Armed Forces between the Korean and early Vietnam conflicts.

M16A1 Rifle—US 5.56MM—The standard rifle of US Armed Forces in Vietnam.

M1911A1—US .45 CALIBER SEMI-AUTOMATIC PISTOL—Standard US Military sidearm for most of the 20th century.

M1928A1 THOMPSON SUBMACHINE GUN .45 CAL. ACP

M60 MACHINE GUN—US 7.62mm belt-fed machine gun.

SKS45 RIFLE—Soviet made, semi-automatic rifle 7.62 x 39mm and was replaced by the AK-47.

☙ MORTARS, GRENADE LAUNCHERS, ARTILLERY, MINES

BM37 82MM MORTAR—Soviet made, medium-duty mortar. Chinese version is Type-53. Used by NVA in Vietnam.

M101A1 HOWITZER—105mm light field artillery piece. Old designation, M2A1.

M107 SELF-PROPELLED GUN—175mm self-propelled artillery gun used for long-range fire support.

M18 RECOILLESS RIFLE—A 57mm shoulder-fired, anti-tank recoilless rifle that was used by the US Army in World War II and the Korean War. (Wikipedia)

M18A1 CLAYMORE ANTI-PERSONNEL MINE—A directional mine with a plastic housing containing C-4 explosive and steel buck shot set into an epoxy resin, primarily fired with a handheld detonator. Several of these mines can be wired in a series called a "daisy chain." (Wikipedia)

M195 20MM AUTOMATIC GUN—Gatling-type rotary cannon used by the United States military mounted on the AH-Cobra Gunship et al. (Wikipedia)

M2 4.2 INCH MORTAR or 107mm—A US mortar used primarily during WWII and Korea. Also used by ARVN troops (South Vietnam). It was unusual for a mortar because it had a rifled barrel.

M2 MORTAR or 60MM—A lightweight mortar used by US troops in Vietnam. A Chinese version was used by the NVA.

M20A1 BAZOOKA (and variants) 3.5 INCH or 90 MM—A shoulder-fired, rocket-propelled grenade launcher.

M203 40 MM GRENADE LAUNCHER—Mounted to an M16A1 rifle. Uses same rounds as the M79.

M252 81MM MORTAR —Old designation: L-16 81MM MORTAR

M26 FRAGMENTATION GRENADE—US hand grenade used during the Korean and Vietnam Wars.

M40 106MM RECOILLESS RIFLE W/ M8C .50 CAL. SINGLE-BARREL SPOTTER RIFLE

M79 40×46MM GRENADE LAUNCHER—Handheld launcher resembling a large, single-barrel shotgun. (See M203)

MDW—MILITARY DISTRICT OF WASHINGTON

MACHETE—Long, wide, sharp-bladed knife used for clearing jungle vegetation.

MEDEVAC CHOPPER—Army helicopter (primarily Hueys) used to transport wounded to the hospital.

MIKE FORCE—MOBILE STRIKE FORCE—CIDG troops under Special Forces guidance, usually sent out as a reaction force on missions that were particularly dangerous.

MONKEY STRAPS—A harness to keep the door gunner from falling out of his helicopter.

MONSOON RAINS—The rainy phase of seasonal weather caused by changes in atmospheric circulation, etc.

MONTAGNARDS or DEGAR—Indigenous tribes living in the highlands of Vietnam.

MORSE CODE—A method of communication using a series of dots and dashes. Named after Samuel Morse, one of the inventors of the telegraph.

N

NAUTICAL TWILIGHT—Twilight is when the sun has disappeared below the horizon, but its light is still visible to light up the sky. Nautical twilight is when the larger, brighter stars first become visible, making it possible for sailors to navigate at sea.

NVA—NORTH VIETNAMESE ARMY

NUOC MAM—A condiment made of fermented fish sauce, popular in Vietnam.

O

OH-13 HELICOPTER—The Bell-13 Sioux is a three-seat observation helicopter used in the 1950s and early 60s, recognizable by its acrylic "bubble" canopy. (Wikipedia)

OCS—OFFICER CANDIDATE SCHOOL

OP—OBSERVATION POST—See LISTENING POST.

OPERATION NEW ARRIVALS—US military operation from April 29th to September 16th, 1975 to relocate 130,000 Vietnamese refugees to the United States.

OPERATION POWER PACK—A US military intervention in the Dominican Civil War between April and September, 1965, ordered by President Lyndon Johnson to evacuate US citizens and prevent the situation from turning into another Cuban-style revolution.

ORTT—ORGANIZATIONAL READINESS TRAINING TEST

P

PATHFINDER—Specialized infantry soldiers inserted into remote areas to establish landing zones for air assaults and other helicopter operations. (Wikipedia)

PEDALS—Floor pedals on a helicopter. Controls the direction of travel (yaw rate). See CYCLIC and COLLECTIVE.

PETER PILOT—The copilot in a Huey Helicopter.

PIASTERS—Vietnamese money.

PLF—PARACHUTE LANDING FALL—A safety technique used to help parachutists land without being injured.

POLICE CALL—A military formation assembled for the purpose of picking up trash and debris on military property.

PRC-25 or AN/PRC-25—Battery powered backpack radio carried by US soldiers in Vietnam, sometimes referred to as a "prick."

PUFF THE MAGIC DRAGON or SPOOKY—In Vietnam, a weapons system consisting of three GE rotary miniguns, each having six barrels mounted to a C-47 fixed-wing aircraft (re-designated AC-47), capable of firing 50 to 100 rounds per second. The "A" stood for "attack." The AC-47 could fly at a speed of 120 KPH and lay down a barrage of 7.62mm bullets in every square foot across a swath of ground the width of a football field.

R

REDLEG—Slang term for an artilleryman.

R&R—REST AND RELAXATION—Time off given to soldiers for rest and diversion.

RIF—REDUCTION IN FORCE—Involuntary separation from the service to reduce the number of soldiers no longer needed.

ROTC—RESERVE OFFICER TRAINING CORPS

RPG—ROCKET-PROPELLED GRENADE—A shoulder-fired missile weapon that launches rockets equipped with an explosive warhead. (Wikipedia)

RTO—RADIOTELEPHONE OPERATOR—Same as Commo Man.

RVN—REPUBLIC OF VIETNAM

S

SF—SPECIAL FORCES (GREEN BERETS)

SLICK—UH-1 Huey Helicopter used primarily for transporting troops and supplies. "Slicks" usually had only minimal defensive armaments such as a door gunner.

SLICKS AND GUNS—*Slicks* were Huey helicopters with primarily *defensive weapons* and minimal armaments. *Guns* were attack helicopters with *offensive weapons* such as the "B" and later model Hueys and the AH-1 Cobra Gunship. (See M195 20 MM AUTOMATIC GUN)

SNAKE EATER—A term of comradery used among Special Forces soldiers.

SNEAKY PETE—Slang for a Special Forces qualified soldier.

SOP—STANDARD OPERATING PROCEDURE

SPOOKY—SEE PUFF THE MAGIC DRAGON

STRAF—STRATEGIC ARMY FORCES

STRIKE FORCE—A unit consisting of CIDG troops sent out to perform a combat mission. Individual troops in a strike force are called "strikers."

T

TANGLEFOOT—A meshwork of barbed wire strung out along the ground to make it difficult to walk across without getting tangled up. Used primarily for perimeter defense.

TDY—TEMPORARY DUTY—An assignment to perform temporary duty away from your regularly assigned station.

TOP—TOP SGT—Slang term for the first sergeant.

V

VFR—VISUAL FLIGHT RULES—Flying by eye sight without instrumentation.

VNSF—VIETNAMESE SPECIAL FORCES—Same as LLDB.

VC or VIET CONG—Irregular or indigenous troops under the leadership of the Communist North Vietnamese Army.

W

WAR ZONE D—War Zone D was the area in South Vietnam around the Dong Nai River, north of Bien Hoa which served as a Viet Cong (VC) and People's Army of Vietnam (PAVN) base area and infiltration route during the Vietnam War. (Wikipedia)

WP—WHITE PHOSPHORUS—A highly flammable substance used in grenades, mortars, and artillery rounds. Slang terms e.g., Willie Pete and Whiskey Papa.

BIOS

Colonel Nicholas John Hun was born in Budapest, Hungary, on January 26th, 1942 and entered the United States Army from Cleveland, Ohio in 1961. He served in various airborne units until he was commissioned through Infantry Officer Candidate School in 1966.

Colonel Hun's first commissioned assignment was as an A Team commander with the 10th Special Forces in Germany. In Vietnam with the 5th Special Forces, he served as executive officer to A-342 in Camp Dong Xoai and as executive officer in A-344 in Camp Bunard, followed by a tour as a platoon commander with Company B, 2nd Battalion, 173rd Airborne Brigade. Upon returning to CONUS, he was assigned a basic training company at Fort Lewis, Washington.

After completing flight school in 1969, he returned to Vietnam to the 145th Combat Aviation Battalion as an attack helicopter platoon commander. He next served as senior army instructor at Massanutten Military Academy, Woodstock, Virginia until 1974 when he transferred to Fort Hood, Texas as commander of the 411th MP Company, and then to the 720th Military Police Battalion as S-3 officer.

Colonel Hun's next assignment was as deputy provost marshal at the United States Military Academy, West Point, New York, which was followed by a tour as provost marshal in Fort Myer, Virginia. Prior to assuming command of the 3rd Battalion, United States Army Correctional Activity, Colonel Hun served two years in Panama as the deputy commander of law enforcement activity, 193rd Infantry Brigade. Colonel Hun's next assignment was as commander of the Columbus Recruiting Battalion in Ohio after his assignment at Fort

Riley, Kansas and later as senior army advisor to the West Virginia Army National Guard.

Retired from the army, Colonel Hun was appointed commissioner of corrections in 1992 for West Virginia. Later, he became a team leader for the Veterans Administration at the Huntington Vet Center. Currently, he is in business as a private investigator and as a consultant for several national companies.

Colonel Hun is a graduate of the Infantry Officer Advanced Course, 1971; the Military Police Officer Transition Course, 1974; and the Command and General Staff College, 1982.

He received his bachelor's degree from the University of Nebraska in 1972 and a master's degree in counseling from Long Island University in 1978.

Among Colonel Hun's decorations are the Distinguished Flying Cross, the Bronze Star with "V" and three oak leaf clusters, the Meritorious Service Medal with three oak leaf clusters, and the Purple Heart. Also, he received the Vietnamese Cross of Gallantry with Silver Star.

☙

Michael Leonard Jewell is an indie author/publisher, writer of

historical fiction, and a sometime poet. He was born near Sodus, Michigan, where he now resides with his wife Rita. He served in the army as a military policeman, attended college in Indiana majoring in pastoral theology, and is a retired public safety 911 dispatcher for Berrien County, Michigan. Mike is a member of the Western Writers of America and is also one of Colonel Hun's soldiers.

WARRIOR'S WORDS

Words from some of the men who have borne
the battle just as they wrote them.

WELCOME HOME

by Phillip E. Crowell

In '67, "welcome home" was never heard,
My uniform, badge of courage was just a word.
Life was "topsy-turvy" and no one cared or knew,
The fight, fear, sorrow and suffering we'd all been through.

We looked for a job only to be scorned,
As murderers, rapists, child killers and devils with horns.
Some of us bought into that guilt and shame,
While the stronger never played that game.

We'd gone down that road our country prescribed,
Only to be sidetracked by our nation's divide.
We trusted no one and fought for ourselves,
Sometimes with meaningless jobs to put food on our shelves.

Some married, some didn't, it really didn't matter,
The name calling followed us, we were as mad as the Hatter.
It took years of fighting with demons to gain insight,
That most all were wounded no matter which fight.

Whether here or there the nightmares would follow,
And carve out our essence until most were hollow.
We fought for our Country, a war of their choosing,
And took the brunt of their politics until they chose losing.

Both sides of the sword ran through our hearts,
Whether here at home, in the bunkers or on the ramparts.
Today, I recall the friends I have lost,
Most suffering from wounds not in combat but of political cost.

Today, I can hold my head high and look toward the sun,
Knowing full well we won the battles at full run.
After 10 years of war, some may echo this poem,
And to all of you I say "Welcome Home!"

Stand down soldier, your job well done,
Hell is over and its Heaven to come!

WELCOME HOME

ଔ

A BRUISED AND PURPLE HEART

by John P. Goodwin

As I walked into the room
I gazed upon the wall
At a yellowed piece of paper
That soon would tell it all

The story of a young man
Who served and done his part
Above the yellowed paper
Hung a tattered purple heart

As the story unfolded
It told of bravery in a land afar
Beside the yellowed paper
Hung a tarnished bronze star

Across the room
Sat a man of forty-three
Who talked of life and death
And what it cost to keep us free

He said that's where they get color
As a teardrop left his eye
It's hard to feel and see the pain
And watch your brothers die

And then be rejected by your country
For only doing your part
And how deeply this had bruised
His already purple heart

There are thousands of vets
Whose stories are the same
Who fought for God and Country
Not an armchair warrior's game

They live all around you
Each with their own story to tell
You see their bodies daily
But their minds are still in hell

For they still fight an enemy
But this time it lives within
Not knowing what was for freedom
Or what was just a sin

Their every move is questioned
What was right and what was wrong
Their days are seldom normal
And their sleepless nights are long

They would like to be a part of life
But feel so far away
Instead of living life to live
It's just surviving day to day

Now that you know
What sets these vets apart
Remember they will carry with them
Till their dying day a bruised and purple heart

Let's all learn a lesson
Give respect when and where it's due
For their blood flowed like water
On a foreign soil for freedom me and you

A BRUISED AND PURPLE HEART

☙

A THOUSAND YARD STARE

By John P. Goodwin

Come take a trip
In my mind if you care
And see what's been seen
By a thousand-yard stare

A buddy in pain
Another that's dying
In the pitch-black night
Others are crying

Some for their god
Some for their mother
And all we can do
Is look at each other

And wait for the dark
To be met by the light
And hope and pray
That's the end of the fight

Chopper ours out
Pile up their dead
Through all this
Not much is said

Get your camera out
Take a picture of some
Say cheese m************
Out of luck you have run

Go through your buddy's pack
Get what you can take
Maybe you'll find
Some peaches and pound cake

Saddle up
Is what I heard the gunny say
Yes you're in the Nam
And it's a brand-new day

Set the hill on fire
So their bodies will burn
The smell of it all
Makes my stomach turn

As I walk away
I don't even look back
I just cuss the weight
Of this damned old ruck sack

I carry these memories home
And store them away
But they come back to haunt me
At the end of each day

They dance through my mind
All during the night
And again I pray
For the end of the fight

I awaken quickly
And realize it's no longer real
But I'm sweating and shaking
From the fear that I feel

I get out of bed
To dry my body and hair
And as I look in the mirror
I see a thousand-yard stare.

ଓ

SOLDIER'S SONG

By Nicholas J. Hun

When I was a young man, about eighteen,
I enlisted in the service, off to follow a dream,
I enlisted in the service, a soldier boy to be,
To hear those muskets rattling and to see what I could see.

I followed the sounds of distant thunder, kept my head down in the rain,
Knowing freedom must be earned again, again and again,
I have seen exotic places, felt the terror and the pain,
Never thinking was it worth it, just to see Old Glory again.

I watched as the wall crumbled and I have seen the tyrant run,
I'm proud of what we fought for—our freedom in the sun,
Along the way I have seen some things, I wish I hadn't seen,

I have some wounds that will not heal, I'll take them to Fiddler's Green.

When the battlefield lies silent and the smoke has cleared away,
Only long white lines of marble remind us—we were there.
The years have brought my family, a woman steady and true,
A nation that stands sovereign, thanks to men like me and you.

Though my youth has long since vanished to gentle shades of gray,
My hand is strong and steady, I'm a soldier to this day,
If ever my country needs a man—a trooper I remain,
I'll pull out my boots and helmet and I'll hit the silk again,
I'll pull out my boots and helmet and I'll hit the silk again.

SOLDIER'S SONG

ꙮ

YOU HAVE SURVIVED ANOTHER DAY

by Nicholas J. Hun

Mud is on your boots today
A scorpion you brush away
Another day at outpost one
Another wild run to the sun
The RPG flash fill the air
You hear the swoosh, you see the trail
You respond with lightning speed
Hot casings pile high at your feet

You won't live another day
Unless you blow them all away
You don't care what's right or wrong
You only know, you must be strong
In your mind, you hear a song
It takes you back where you belong
Shadows pass outside your door
You set your switch on rock and roll
You pull the trigger all the way
You dodge the lead, coming your way
You scream out an obscenity
As you waste what you cannot see
You smell the cordite in the air
You see the bodies lying there
The battle ends before it starts
No need to count the body parts
You move on at crazy speed
You never see the kid in the street
Another friend has died today
A chopper lands, takes him away
Your new best friend is your M-4
You feel like you have been here before
Your weariness seems far away
You have survived another day

FROM SHAKESPEARE'S HENRY V

"Whoever does not have the stomach for this fight, let him depart. Give him money to speed his departure, since we wish not to die in that's man's company. Whoever lives past today and comes home safely will rouse himself every year on this day, show his neighbor his scars, and tell embellished stories of all their great feats of battle. These stories he will teach his son and from this day until the end of the world we shall be remembered. We few, we happy few, we band of brothers; for whoever has shed his blood with me shall be my brother. And those men afraid to go will think themselves lesser men as they hear of how we fought and died together."

—Henry V, Act IV, Scene 3

CPSIA information can be obtained
at www.ICGtesting.com
Printed in the USA
BVHW010214140621
609519BV00010B/442